WHY EVERY ENTREPRENEUR MUST WRITE A BOOK

How to use a Book as a Strategy (BaaS) for Influence, Income & Impact

RAAM ANAND

STARDOM BOOKS
www.StardomBooks.com

STARDOM BOOKS
112 Bordeaux Ct.
Coppell, TX 75019, USA

Copyright © 2025 by Raam Anand

All rights reserved. No part of this book may be reproduced or used in any manner without written permission of the copyright owner except for the use of quotations in a book review.

FIRST EDITION APRIL 2025

STARDOM BOOKS, LLC.
112 Bordeaux Ct. Coppell, TX 75019, USA

www.stardombooks.com

Stardom Books, United States
Stardom Alliance, India

The author and publishers have made all reasonable efforts to contact copyright holders for permission and apologize for any omissions or errors in the form of credits given. Corrections may be made to future editions.

Why Every Entrepreneur Must Write a Book
How to use a Book as a Strategy (BaaS) for Influence, Income & Impact

Raam Anand

p. 167
cm. 13.97 X 21.59

Category: LAN027000 LANGUAGE ARTS & DISCIPLINES/ Publishers & Publishing Industry
BUS071000 BUSINESS & ECONOMICS/ Leadership

ISBN:978-1-957456-64-5

DEDICATION

To the architects of change and shepherds of innovation, To the stewards of corporate citadels and the captains of industry, This book is dedicated to you— The Founders who sculpt the future with the decisions of today, The guardians of growth, the heralds of progress, And the ever-curious minds who recognize the pen as mighty. May this volume inspire you to chart new territories, in business, in leadership, and in the narratives you choose to share.

CONTENTS

ACKNOWLEDGMENTS	VI
INTRODUCTION	1
1. ELEVATING YOUR PROFESSIONAL STATUS	7
2. OVERCOMING INNER BARRIERS TO AUTHORSHIP	19
3. EXPANDING YOUR PROFESSIONAL NETWORK	23
4. ENHANCING STAKEHOLDER RELATIONSHIPS	33
5. BOOSTING YOUR BRAND'S REPUTATION	41
6. PERSONAL AND PROFESSIONAL FULFILLMENT	55
7. HANDLING CRITICISM, FEEDBACK, AND PUBLIC REACTION	69
8. STRATEGIC BUSINESS GROWTH	83
9. MONETIZING YOUR BOOK BEYOND ROYALTIES	95
10. HOW TO ACHIEVE THIS DREAM OUTCOME	111
11. GOING GLOBAL: REACHING INTERNATIONAL AUDIENCES AND MARKETS	129
12. PUTTING IT ALL TOGETHER	141
BONUS:	151
NEXT STEPS...	159
ABOUT THE AUTHOR	161

ACKNOWLEDGMENTS

Gratitude is the heart's memory, and this book pulses with appreciation for many. To my family, for their patience and belief in the power of storytelling, I am forever grateful.

My sincerest thanks to the cadre of peers and mentors from boardrooms to the school of hard-knocks, whose experiences and insights have been the bedrock of my journey. I extend my profound appreciation to the team at Stardom Books, warrants a special mention for their strategic support and steadfast accountability that steered this project to its completion.

For the leaders who shared their time and narratives, and to you, the reader, embarking on this written voyage, may you find in these pages the spark to ignite your own author ambitions.

In dedication to those who dare to lead not just in practice but also on paper, may this book serve as a beacon and a bridge to your next big leap.

INTRODUCTION

"Information is the oxygen of the modern age."
—**Ronald Reagan**

In the dynamic and highly competitive world of startups and entrepreneurship, founders are constantly seeking innovative ways to gain a competitive edge, establish authority, and make a lasting impact. One powerful yet often overlooked strategy is writing a book. This book, "***Why Every Entrepreneur Must Write A Book:** How to use a Book as a Strategy (Baas) for Influence, Income & Impact*" aims to demystify the process of book writing for entrepreneurs and illustrate how becoming an author can significantly elevate your professional status, expand your network, enhance stakeholder relationships, boost your startup's reputation, and contribute to personal and professional fulfillment.

Writing a book might seem like an insurmountable task, especially for those already juggling the grid responsibilities of running a startup. However, this book will guide you through the step-by-step process, from conceptualizing your idea to seeing your book in print. **We'll also address potential challenges you might face and provide strategies to overcome them.** By the end, you'll understand not only the mechanics of writing and publishing but also the strategic benefits that come with being a published author.

Why Writing a Book is Beneficial for Entrepreneurs

Entrepreneurs and especially startups, need funding. A book is an excellent investment in seeking financing because it will instantly make the author an authority on the topic. Investors want to invest their money with 'experts' and not rookies. Startups and entrepreneurs should create a book to build their brand and attract the right support for their ideas.

In today's information age, content is king. For startup founders, a book can serve as a powerful tool to convey your vision, share your expertise, and differentiate yourself from your competition. Here are a few reasons why writing a book can be particularly beneficial:

1. Establishing Authority and Credibility: A book can position you as a thought leader in your industry. It serves as a testament to your knowledge and expertise, enhancing your credibility with investors, clients, and peers.

2. Networking Opportunities: Authors often find that their books open doors to new professional connections, speaking engagements, and collaborative ventures. Your book can act as a conversation starter, helping you to build relationships with influential figures in your field.

3. Marketing and Branding: A well-written book can be a cornerstone of your marketing strategy, helping to boost your startup's visibility and reputation. It can also provide material for content marketing, media coverage, and public relations efforts.

4. Personal and Professional Fulfillment: Writing a book is a significant personal achievement that can bring a sense of fulfillment and pride. **It's not just about the book; it's about the personal growth and learning curve that comes with the process.** It allows you to share your journey, leave a legacy, and contribute to entrepreneurial literature.

5. Strategic Business Growth: A book can drive strategic business growth by generating leads, attracting new clients, and creating additional revenue streams through book sales, speaking engagements, and consulting opportunities.

Overview of How this Book Will Help

This book is structured to provide you with a comprehensive roadmap for writing and publishing your own book. Each chapter focuses on a specific aspect of the process and the strategic benefits of authorship. Here's a brief overview of what you can expect:

- **Chapter 1:** *Elevating Your Professional Status:* Learn how a book can establish your authority and credibility in the startup ecosystem.
- **Chapter 2:** *Overcoming Inner Barriers to Authorship:* Identify and conquer the self-doubts, fears, and mindset challenges that are holding you back from writing and publishing your book.
- **Chapter 3:** *Expanding Your Professional Network:* Discover how a book can open doors to new connections and opportunities.
- **Chapter 4:** *Enhancing Stakeholder Relationships:* Understand how a book can improve communication and build trust with investors and clients.
- **Chapter 5:** *Boosting Your Startup's Reputation:* Explore how a book can be a powerful marketing and branding tool.
- **Chapter 6:** *Personal and Professional Fulfillment: Reflect on the personal satisfaction and legacy-building aspects of becoming a published author.*
- **Chapter 7:** *Handling Criticism, Feedback and Public Reaction:* Learn how to navigate reviews, critiques, and audience responses constructively, turning feedback into an opportunity for growth and credibility.
- **Chapter 8:** *Strategic Business Growth:* See how a book can drive business growth through lead generation and new revenue streams.
- **Chapter 9:** *Monetizing Your Book Beyond Royalties:* Explore various strategies to generate revenue from your book.
- **Chapter 10:** *How To Achieve this Dream Outcome:* Learn about the comprehensive support services available to help you succeed in your authorship journey.
- **Chapter 11:** *Going Global: Reaching International Audiences and Markets:* Understand how to expand your book's reach beyond local markets to connect with a global readership.

Throughout the book, you'll find real-life examples, anecdotes, research, and citations that underscore the transformative power of authorship.

Realizing the Potential of Becoming a Published Author

Consider the journey of Eric Ries, author of "The Lean Startup." Before his book became a bestseller, Ries was known within certain circles as a startup advisor and entrepreneur. However, the publication of "The Lean Startup" catapulted him to global recognition, establishing him as a leading authority on startup methodology. His book not only provided invaluable insights to countless entrepreneurs but also opened up numerous opportunities for speaking engagements, consulting gigs, and media appearances.

Similarly, Ben Horowitz, co-founder of Andreessen Horowitz, wrote "The Hard Thing About Hard Things," sharing his experiences and insights on building and running startups. This book not only solidified his reputation as a thought leader but also became a key resource for entrepreneurs facing the challenges of scaling their businesses.

These examples illustrate the potential impact of becoming a published author. By sharing your knowledge and experiences in a book, you can significantly enhance your professional profile and influence within your industry.

Understanding the Strategic Advantages of Authorship

One of the strategic advantages of writing a book is the ability to control your narrative. In the fast-paced startup world, where perceptions can shift rapidly, having a book allows you to shape how you are perceived by investors, clients, and peers. It provides a platform for you to articulate your vision, share your insights, and establish your expertise.

Moreover, a book can serve as a powerful marketing tool. Unlike blog posts or social media updates, a book has a lasting presence. It can be shared, referenced, and cited long after its publication. This longevity helps build a sustained personal brand and keeps your ideas in circulation within the industry.

For instance, Tony Hsieh, the late CEO of Zappos, wrote "Delivering Happiness" to share his philosophy on customer service and company culture. The book not only helped to solidify Zappos' brand but also positioned Hsieh as a thought leader in business culture and customer satisfaction. His book continues to be a key resource for entrepreneurs and business leaders around the world.

Case Study: The Journey of an Entrepreneur

Consider the journey of Rand Fishkin, co-founder of Moz and author of "Lost and Founder." Fishkin's book provides an honest, behind-the-scenes look at the realities of startup life, offering valuable lessons for aspiring entrepreneurs. Writing the book allowed Fishkin to share his experiences, establish his authority, and build a deeper connection with his audience. The book also opened up new opportunities for speaking engagements and consulting work, further enhancing his professional profile.

The Importance of Sharing Your Story

Your journey as a startup founder is unique. The challenges you've faced, the lessons you've learned, and the successes you've achieved can provide invaluable insights to others. By writing a book, you have the opportunity to share your story and contribute to the entrepreneurial community. Your book can inspire, educate, and empower other founders, helping them navigate their own startup journeys.

Writing a book is a powerful strategy for startup founders looking to elevate their professional status, expand their network, enhance stakeholder relationships, boost their startup's reputation, and achieve personal and professional fulfillment. This book will guide you through the process, providing you with the tools and insights you need to succeed. So, let's embark on this journey together and unlock the transformative power of becoming a published author.

So, what are you waiting for?

Turn the page over, and let's get reading!

> *"When you speak, your words live for that moment. When you write, your words live forever."*
> — **Robin Sharma**

> **Key Takeaways**
>
> As you begin this journey of writing and publishing your own book, here are a few key takeaways to keep in mind:
>
> - **Authorship as a Strategy:** Writing a book is not just about sharing your knowledge; it's a strategic move that can enhance your professional status, expand your network, and drive business growth.
>
> - **Long-term Benefits:** The benefits of writing a book extend far beyond its publication. A book can have a lasting impact on your career, your startup, and your personal fulfillment.
>
> - **Support and Resources:** You don't have to navigate this journey alone. There are numerous resources and support services available to help you succeed in your authorship journey.
>
> - **Start Now:** The process of writing a book can seem daunting, but the first step is to start. This book will guide you through each stage of the process, providing you with the tools and insights you need to succeed.

A book immortalizes your expertise and keeps working for you long after you've written it.

1

ELEVATING YOUR PROFESSIONAL STATUS

"The secret of getting ahead is getting started."
—**Mark Twain**

In the high-stakes world of startups, credibility and authority can make or break a venture. Picture yourself at a prestigious startup conference surrounded by potential investors and partners. The keynote speaker, a well-known startup founder, takes the stage. As they begin to speak, the title of their bestselling book is prominently displayed on the screen behind them. The room is captivated, and it's clear that this founder's book has established their status as an authority in the industry.

This scene is not an uncommon occurrence; many successful startup founders have used authorship as a strategic tool to elevate their professional status.

Writing a book can significantly enhance your professional credibility and position you as a thought leader within your industry. This chapter delves into how a book can establish your authority, boost your credibility, and set you apart from the competition.

Establishing Authority

One of the most compelling reasons startup founders write a book is to establish their authority in the field. A book serves as a tangible representation of your expertise and insights, offering readers a deep dive into your knowledge and experiences. In an industry where authority can significantly influence success, a book can be a powerful differentiator, solidifying your position as a thought leader.

It is a widespread opinion that "a book is the new business card." However, I am of the dissenting opinion because just about anyone can have a business card. You could go to a print shop and get business cards, but you cannot just author a book at a print shop. What I like to say instead is that "your own book is the new college degree."

Four decades ago, only about 10 percent of people could actually go to college. A college degree was an indication of credibility and authority. However, college degrees aren't exclusive anymore; they do not carry the same gravitas they once did. So, what can be considered as a sign of credibility and authority today while also maintaining authenticity and uniqueness?

Getting your book published, of course!

Writing a book shows that you have the courage to put your thoughts out there that you can commit to and follow through with that commitment. It shows that you are the type to get things done, things that are hard and prestigious and involve a great deal of effort and persistence. Most people do not have it within themselves to take that risk: to set themselves up to be scrutinized and to show the world what they stand for.

Publishing a book is one of the best ways of getting attention and gaining trust; it is a multipurpose marketing tool. Your book can help you with almost anything you want: sales, media publicity, word-of-mouth publicity, recognition as an authority, etc.

Let's explore a few advantages of writing a book...but before that, let me indulge you with some light statistics. Roughly less than 10% of successful startup founders have authored books. This estimate is derived from examining lists of top entrepreneurs and cross-referencing published works.

As a founder, you are not only the leader but have also been the jack-of-all-trades, handling tasks from typing and answering phones to accounting and tech support. Despite these initial challenges, you have, like many other founders, still reached impressive heights in your career.

With more people aspiring to become startup founders, the market for founder-authored books is becoming increasingly vibrant. The number of founders who write books is relatively small compared to the total number of entrepreneurs, but those who do often make a significant impact with their writings.

Books written by founders often become bestsellers and are highly influential in the business and entrepreneurial communities. They serve as valuable guides and sources of inspiration for aspiring entrepreneurs. While a minority of founders write books, those who do often provide valuable insights and inspiration to the broader entrepreneurial community.

For instance, Reid Hoffman, co-founder of LinkedIn, co-authored "The Startup of You" with Ben Casnocha. The book explores the mindset and strategies professionals can adopt to navigate the modern career landscape. By sharing his insights and experiences, Hoffman has cemented his status as a thought leader, expanding his influence beyond the tech world. His book has been referenced in numerous business discussions, used in educational curricula, and cited by professionals across various industries.

The process of writing a book requires a deep understanding of your subject matter. As you research and organize your thoughts, you also tend to gain a more nuanced perspective of your field. This intellectual rigor translates into the content of your book, which readers will recognize and appreciate. Your book becomes a testament to your expertise. This perceived authority can open doors to new opportunities, from speaking engagements to advisory roles, leaving you with a deep sense of pride, accomplishment, and the feeling of being truly respected in your field.

How a Book Positions You as a Thought Leader

Forbes describes the term 'thought leader' as "an individual or firm that prospects, clients, referral sources, intermediaries, and even competitors recognize as one of the foremost authorities in selected areas of specialization, resulting in its being the go-to individual or organization for said expertise." A thought leader drives change and steers trends. The keyword here is '**authority**,' and authority, quite literally, comes from being an author, right?

The term 'thought leader' or the concept has been around for ages. However, since the dawn of the Internet, the word has found a new meaning. The thought leaders today are entrepreneurs, motivational speakers, or influencers. You are called a thought leader if you are wise and have quick decision-making skills. You are the go-to person and have the authority to address various concerns.

Given the current times when so many things are constantly unfolding around us, all people need is a little bit of positivity. Thought leaders provide that. Thought leaders bring hope and help to their followers in a big way. Being a thought leader means being recognized as an expert whose opinions and insights are sought after and valued. Writing a book is one of the most effective ways to position yourself as a thought leader. It allows you to share your unique perspective on industry trends, challenges, and future directions. Moreover, it gives you a platform to introduce new concepts and frameworks that can shape the thinking of others, inspiring you to make a meaningful contribution to your industry.

Writing a book also provides a structured format to comprehensively articulate your ideas and insights. Unlike articles or blog posts, a book allows for a more in-depth exploration of topics, enabling you to present your thoughts in a detailed and cohesive manner. This thoroughness is appreciated by readers and contributes to your reputation as a knowledgeable and reliable source of information. So, a book written by a thought leader is highly valued.

Ries' journey illustrates the transformative power of authorship. By writing a book, he was able to share his innovative ideas with a global audience, significantly enhancing his professional reputation and influence. His book continues to be a key resource for entrepreneurs, demonstrating the lasting impact that authorship can have on your career.

"Did you know that the average person makes around 35,000 decisions per day? So, are you making decisions that will get you closer to your goals?"

The Rise of Eric Ries

Eric Ries' "The Lean Startup" introduced the concept of the lean startup methodology, which has since become a foundational principle in the startup ecosystem. Before the publication of his book, Ries was known within certain circles as an advocate for lean principles. However, "The Lean Startup" catapulted him to global recognition, establishing him as a leading authority on startup methodology. His ideas have influenced countless entrepreneurs and startups, demonstrating the profound impact that a book can have on establishing thought leadership.

Eric Ries transformed his professional trajectory after publishing "The Lean Startup." Before the book, Ries was primarily known within Silicon Valley circles for his work with IMVU, a 3D avatar-based social network. However, the lean startup methodology he developed during his time at IMVU had yet to reach a broader audience.

Ries decided to write "The Lean Startup" to share his methodology with a wider audience. The book's success was immediate and far-reaching. It not only introduced the concept of validated learning, build-measure-learn feedback loops, and minimum viable products (MVPs) but also became a must-read for entrepreneurs around the world. The lean startup methodology revolutionized how startups approach product development and growth, and Ries became a sought-after speaker and advisor. His book solidified his status as a thought leader and fundamentally changed the startup landscape.

How Being Seen as an Authority Can Impact Your Career

The benefits of being perceived as an authority extend beyond recognition and accolades. Here are some ways that authorship can impact your career:

1. Increased Trust and Credibility: Writing a book on a subject related to your industry displays your deep understanding of the subject matter. It adds credibility to your voice, making you a trusted source of advice and guidance. The comprehensive nature of a book will allow you to delve into complex topics, providing in-depth analysis that further enhances your credibility.

Investors, clients, and partners are likelier to trust someone whose expertise is demonstrated through a published book. This increased trust can lead to more opportunities for funding, partnerships, and collaborations.

2. Speaking Engagements: A book can bring you to the attention of a wider audience, including potential clients, collaborators, or even the media. It can lead to speaking engagements, interviews, and other opportunities for exposure. Increased visibility enhances your professional reputation and opens doors to new avenues of growth and recognition. Writing allows you to showcase your knowledge and expertise in a particular field. You can establish your credibility by sharing your insights, experiences, and research findings within your domain. Your written works provide evidence of your depth of understanding and can contribute to building your reputation as a thought leader. Thought leaders are often invited to speak at conferences, seminars, and industry events. These speaking engagements can further enhance your visibility and reputation, allowing you to reach a broader audience.

3. Media Coverage: As an author, you are more likely to be approached by journalists and media outlets for interviews and commentary. This media coverage can amplify your message and reach, helping you to influence public discourse and opinion. When a media outlet wants a comment on something, whose opinion do they solicit? Obviously, they ask the experts. And how do they know if someone is an expert? They recognize experts by the books they have authored.

4. Advisory and Board Roles: Established authorities are frequently invited to join advisory boards and take on mentorship roles. These positions not only provide additional income streams but also allow you to shape the direction of other startups and ventures. The impact on your career can be profound. A published book sets you apart from your peers, positioning you as an industry expert. This heightened visibility and recognition attract significant career opportunities, like board invitations, high-level consulting engagements, or the chance to take on more influential leadership roles. Another significant benefit is that it will also greatly expand your scope, and it will increase your exposure within the community as well. Soon, organizations will begin contacting you as the go-to expert in your field. Once you feel that you have built up enough experience, take to the road. When you have published a book and established yourself as a reputable SME in the local media and your community, your reach tends to expand.

5. Networking Opportunities: The process of publishing and promoting a book can help you expand your professional network. Engaging with readers, fellow experts, and industry professionals through book events, conferences, and online platforms can lead to valuable connections. These connections can result in partnerships, collaborations, and business opportunities that further enhance your career trajectory. Writing also allows you to connect with like-minded individuals, experts, and influencers in your field. Through collaborations, joint publications, and contributions to collective works, you can leverage your networks to amplify your reach, exchange ideas, and gain further credibility within your communities.

The program managers of some of the most prestigious arenas you would love to enter, like lecture halls, television studios, boardrooms, social media pages, etc., regularly seek and solicit authors as speakers. Becoming a published author opens up a number of incredible opportunities in the long run. As an author, you gain access to exclusive networks and communities of other thought leaders and influencers. These connections can lead to new partnerships, collaborations, and opportunities for growth.

Building Credibility

Writing has always been influenced and shaped by human needs, trends, and a plethora of societal factors throughout history. Its evolution has been intertwined with many aspects of life, including law, commerce, business, education, religion, storytelling, and politics. As writing permeated these domains, it adapted and transformed to meet the specific requirements and purposes of each.

Politics, in particular, has played a significant role in shaping the trajectory of writing throughout history. Governments and ruling powers have recognized the power of the written word to disseminate information, shape public opinion, and exert control. Political motivations have often driven changes in writing systems, scripts, and language policies. Influential people have always gained credibility after writing through various mechanisms, demonstrating their expertise, insights, and thought leadership.

However, the power of writing is not exclusive to those in positions of authority only. Influential people from all walks of life have harnessed the transformative potential of writing to gain credibility, express their opinions, share their expertise, and leave their mark on the world. Writing provides a unique platform for everyone to showcase their insights, thought leadership, and unique perspectives.

Just as other authorities have identified the power of writing, I want to enable you to write and express your opinions, viewpoints, and expertise and make a mark for yourself.

Credibility is a crucial component of success in the startup world. It influences how others perceive your expertise and trustworthiness, which can have a direct impact on your ability to attract investors, clients, and partners. Writing a book is a powerful way to build and enhance your credibility.

Enhancing Investor and Client Trust

Investors and clients are constantly evaluating the credibility of startup founders. A well-written book can serve as a testament to your knowledge and expertise, making it easier to gain their trust and confidence.

Ben Horowitz, co-founder of Andreessen Horowitz, authored "The Hard Thing About Hard Things," which provides a candid look at the challenges of building and running startups, offering valuable insights and practical advice. By sharing his experiences and lessons learned, Horowitz has established himself as a credible and trustworthy expert in the startup world. His book has been praised by entrepreneurs, investors, and business leaders, further enhancing his reputation and credibility.

Horowitz's book is a testament to the power of transparency and authenticity. By openly discussing the difficulties and setbacks he encountered, Horowitz has built a reputation for honesty and integrity. This transparency has resonated with readers, enhancing his credibility and trustworthiness.

In addition to enhancing credibility, a book can also serve as a powerful tool for educating investors and clients. By providing detailed insights into your industry, business model, and vision, your book can help investors and clients understand and appreciate the value of your startup. This increased understanding can lead to stronger relationships and more opportunities for growth.

Differentiating Yourself from Other Startup Founders

In a crowded and competitive startup landscape, standing out can be a significant challenge. Writing a book can differentiate you from other startup founders by showcasing your unique insights and experiences. It sets you apart as someone who has taken the time to reflect on their journey and share their knowledge with others.

A book assumes the role of a dynamic extension of an author's personal brand. The book becomes a tangible embodiment of your values, insights, and experiences, underscoring your distinctiveness in a sea of voices.

Standing Out Through Authorship

Sophia Amoruso, founder of Nasty Gal and the author of "#GIRLBOSS," chronicles her journey from starting an eBay store selling vintage clothing to building a multimillion-dollar fashion empire. By sharing her unconventional path to success, Amoruso has differentiated herself from other fashion entrepreneurs. Her book has resonated with a wide audience, particularly young women aspiring to break into the fashion industry. "#GIRLBOSS" not only elevated Amoruso's profile but also inspired a movement, leading to a Netflix series and a foundation supporting female entrepreneurs.

Amoruso's book demonstrates how authorship can be a powerful tool for differentiation. Before her book, Amoruso was known primarily within niche fashion circles. However, "#GIRLBOSS" catapulted her to mainstream recognition, establishing her as a cultural icon and business leader. The book's success led to a significant expansion of her personal brand, including speaking engagements, media appearances, and the founding of the GIRLBOSS Foundation, which supports women in business.

Amoruso's story illustrates that writing a book can serve as a platform to share your unique story and perspective, setting you apart from the competition. Her book has inspired countless readers and has had a lasting impact on the entrepreneurial community, particularly among women.

The Importance of Sharing Your Story

Your journey as a startup founder is unique. The challenges you've faced, the lessons you've learned, and the successes you've achieved can provide invaluable insights to others. By writing a book, you could have the opportunity to share your story and contribute to the entrepreneurial community. Your book can inspire, educate, and empower other founders, helping them navigate their own startup journeys.

Writing a book is a powerful strategy for startup founders looking to elevate their professional status, expand their network, enhance stakeholder relationships, boost their startup's reputation, and achieve personal and professional fulfillment. This book will guide you through the process, providing you with the tools and insights you need to succeed. So, let's embark on this journey together and unlock the transformative power of becoming a published author.

Numerous studies and expert opinions support the benefits of writing a book for establishing authority and credibility. According to a survey conducted by BookBaby, 83% of business leaders who have written a book reported a significant positive impact on their careers. Additionally, a study published in the Journal of Business Research found that authorship is perceived as a key indicator of expertise and credibility, particularly in knowledge-intensive industries.

Moreover, the Edelman Trust Barometer, an annual global study, consistently highlights the importance of thought leadership in building trust and credibility. The 2021 edition of the study found that 61% of respondents trust individuals who have demonstrated expertise through authored content, such as books and articles.

> **The Journey of Rand Fishkin**
>
> Rand Fishkin, co-founder of Moz, authored "Lost and Founder," which provides an honest, behind-the-scenes look at the realities of startup life, offering valuable lessons for aspiring entrepreneurs. Writing the book allowed Fishkin to share his experiences, establish his authority, and build a deeper connection with his audience. The book also opened up new opportunities for speaking engagements and consulting work, further enhancing his professional profile.
>
> Fishkin's "Lost and Founder" expanded his reach, allowing him to connect with a broader audience of entrepreneurs and business leaders. The book's candid and insightful exploration of startup life resonated with readers, establishing Fishkin as a trusted voice in the entrepreneurial ecosystem.
>
> Fishkin's journey demonstrates that writing a book can be a powerful way to share your story, connect with your audience, and establish your authority. By offering a behind-the-scenes look at the challenges and triumphs of startup life, Fishkin has solidified his reputation as a thought leader and influencer.

According to the Center for Creative Leadership, thought leadership is a critical factor in building trust and credibility. Their research indicates that individuals who are recognized as thought leaders are more likely to be perceived as credible and trustworthy by their peers, clients, and investors. This increased trust can translate into tangible benefits, such as more opportunities for funding, partnerships, and business growth.

Though writing and editing a book requires a fair amount of time and research, it can have transformative results for your business. As you use your book to bolster your credibility and expand your market reach, you will be able to grow at a much faster rate than ever before. By writing a book, entrepreneurs can build their personal brand, establish their expertise, and build trust with potential clients. Your accumulated experience or developed expertise in a specific field holds significant value. It's not always about decades of work; even unique insights gained over intense periods can be highly valuable. Achieving the status of a published author enhances your credibility and authority within your field. It solidifies your expertise, further establishing you as a recognized expert.

Writing a book is a powerful strategy for startup founders looking to establish authority and credibility in their field. By sharing your knowledge and experiences, you can differentiate yourself from the competition, build trust with investors and clients, and open doors to new opportunities for growth. As you embark on this journey, remember that the process of writing a book is not just about sharing what you know; it's about solidifying your place as a thought leader and influencing the future of your industry.

"A positive mindset is essential for success. So, don't forget to practice gratitude and appreciate the little things."

Key Takeaways

- **Authorship as a Differentiator:** Writing a book can set you apart from other startup founders, showcasing your unique insights and experiences.

- **Enhanced Credibility:** A book serves as a testament to your knowledge and expertise, enhancing your credibility with investors, clients, and peers.

- **Opportunities for Growth:** Being seen as an authority can lead to new opportunities for speaking engagements, media coverage, advisory roles, and networking.

2

OVERCOMING INNER BARRIERS TO AUTHORSHIP

"Doubt kills more dreams than failure ever will."
— **Suzy Kassem, Author**

In the world of entrepreneurship, where resourcefulness and resilience are daily necessities, writing a book may still feel like an outsized undertaking. While you may already recognize the strategic benefits of authorship—enhanced credibility, greater influence, and expanded professional networks—there are hidden psychological barriers that prevent many entrepreneurs from fully committing to the process.

This chapter aims to shed light on those inner hurdles and offer practical strategies for overcoming them. By addressing self-doubt, perfectionism, and the perpetual time crunch, you'll gain the mental fortitude to see your book project through to publication.

Understanding the Mental Blocks
Imposter Syndrome: "Who Am I to Write This Book?"

Imposter syndrome can manifest as the nagging feeling that your achievements are unremarkable, and your expertise is inadequate. You might be asking yourself, *"Who am I to advise others?"* Yet paradoxically, the very fact you've navigated unique entrepreneurial challenges—whether they led to success, failure, or a pivot—means you possess valuable insights.

• **Focus on Your Unique Journey**: Even if you haven't built a billion-dollar brand, your personal experiences and learnings can resonate powerfully with readers facing similar obstacles. Your stories connect deeply with your audience and brings in that element of authenticity and transparency to your communication.

• **Shift from Self to Service**: When you concentrate on serving your intended audience—be it fellow entrepreneurs, new business owners, prospects, or peers in your industry—you'll find renewed conviction in what you have to share.

> *"Imposter syndrome doesn't go away—it's something you battle at every level. The trick is to keep showing up anyway."*
> — **James Clear, Author of Atomic Habits**

Perfectionism: The Quest for Flawlessness = Big Dream Killer!

Entrepreneurs often carry high standards of excellence into their writing, sometimes stalling progress in pursuit of a "perfect" final draft. A book is, by nature, an evolving project. Even bestselling authors release revised editions or add new materials as their expertise deepens. That's why you see second and third editions of many books.

• **Set Realistic Milestones**: Break your manuscript into attainable sections or chapters, rather than chasing a pristine final version from the outset.

• **Embrace Iteration**: Remember that revising content is part of the writing journey. A workable first draft is more valuable than a flawless concept kept in your head. Microsoft has known for this technique. Launch the product with a decent fit and then make adjustments in the form of updates in due course (instead of waiting to perfect the product).

Fear of Public Scrutiny

Once you publish your ideas in a book, they become open to praise, critique, and everything in between. The vulnerability of "going on record" can be a common stumbling block for entrepreneurs used to controlling their brand narrative.

• **Value of Authenticity**: Readers connect more deeply with openness about challenges and lessons learned.

• **Acknowledge the Growth Mindset**: Rather than seeing critique as an attack, treat it as data that informs future editions or spin-off projects.

Practical Strategies for Busy Entrepreneurs

Big Idea #1: Time-Management Tactics

• **Create Non-Negotiable Slots**: Block out specific times for your book project in your weekly calendar. If it's not on the calendar, it will never get done.

• **Use Downtime Efficiently**: Consider dictating notes during your commute or outlining chapters while waiting for the next conference call. Breaking the entire project into smaller, manageable modules is a proven technique that we follow at Stardom Books.

Accountability and Support

• **Join an Entrepreneur Authors' Group**: Seek or form a small peer circle where each member shares weekly book project goals and challenges. Stardom Circle (stardomcircle.com) is our support network for aspiring authors.

• **Professional Editing and Coaching**: Engaging a developmental editor or book coach can help you shape ideas, maintain consistent quality, and stay accountable to deadlines.

Big Idea #2: Aligning Authorship with Entrepreneurial Goals

Many entrepreneurs feel torn between the demands of their company and writing a book. However, rather than treating these as competing pursuits, consider how your manuscript can reinforce your business objectives.

- **Focus on Overlapping Themes:** If your company specializes in sustainability, for example, your book can dive deeper into that area, attracting potential clients, partners, or investors aligned with your mission.
- **Build Brand Consistency:** From chapter titles to anecdotes, weave in your core brand messaging to shape a cohesive narrative around your entrepreneurial journey.

"Confidence is key to success. So, believe in yourself and your ability to succeed."

Key Takeaways

- **Acknowledge Inner Challenges**: Recognize that imposter syndrome, perfectionism, and fear of scrutiny are natural barriers, not disqualifications.

- **Progress Over Perfection**: Break the book-writing process into manageable chunks, valuing momentum over flawless execution.

- **Leverage Accountability**: Join or create supportive networks of entrepreneurial authors, and enlist professional help when needed.

- **View Authorship as Strategic Alignment**: Instead of competition for your time, see the writing process as a parallel track that enriches and promotes your business goals.

3

EXPANDING YOUR PROFESSIONAL NETWORK

"The best thing a human being can do is to help another human being know more."
—Charles Munger

In the interconnected world of startups, networking can be the key to unlocking unprecedented opportunities. Imagine attending a bustling industry conference where every conversation has the potential to lead to a new partnership, a groundbreaking idea, or even significant funding. Now, picture yourself as an author at this event.

As you introduce yourself, you hand over a copy of your book. The response is immediate—a spark of interest, a request for a deeper discussion, and an invitation to speak at a panel.

This scenario is not a mere fantasy; it's the reality for many startup founders who have leveraged authorship to dramatically expand their professional network, and it can be your reality too.

Networking Opportunities

A book can serve as an exceptional networking tool, opening doors that might otherwise remain closed. When you publish a book, you create a lasting piece of intellectual property that speaks for you long after you've left the room. It provides a tangible representation of your expertise and offers a starting point for meaningful conversations.

Within the pages of a book lies the power to forge connections. It becomes a conversation starter, an icebreaker that paves the way for meaningful interactions. The book's content can initiate discussions, cultivate relationships, and unravel doors to collaborations, partnerships, and professional liaisons with industry leaders and peers.

And what better prompt for a conversation starter for networking than showcasing your own book on LinkedIn? Your book establishes you as a credible authority in your industry. Professionals prefer networking with other professionals for mutual gain, and authoring a book opens up opportunities that might take multiple business dates to achieve. On LinkedIn, you can share insights from your book, engage in industry discussions, and connect with professionals who have similar interests. This can help you expand your network and attract the attention of influential individuals.

So, if you have authored a book, the dynamics change significantly. There is a good chance that influential individuals have already come across your book through their professional networks. Even if they haven't, simply offering a copy of your book can set you apart. This can transform you from just another attendee into a credible authority in your industry. The influential person now sees you as a unique and valuable connection, increasing the likelihood of further engagement and opportunities, maybe an invitation to their office for more in-depth discussions. The book instantly switches up your position from being another brick on the wall to being the mural over the brick wall. This is the transformative power of networking, where a simple act can change your professional trajectory and open up new doors of opportunity.

The process of publishing and promoting a book can help you engage with readers, fellow experts, and industry professionals through book events, conferences, and online platforms, leading to valuable connections. These connections can result in partnerships, collaborations, and business opportunities that further enhance your career trajectory. Writing also allows you to connect with like-minded individuals, experts, and influencers in your field. Through collaborations, joint publications, and contributions to collective works, you can leverage your networks to amplify your reach, exchange ideas, and gain further credibility within your communities.

Case-Study: Jason Fried and "Rework"

Jason Fried is the co-founder of Basecamp and co-author of "Rework." Before publishing "Rework," Fried and his company were well-respected in certain circles but had not achieved widespread recognition. The book, which challenged conventional business practices and offered new perspectives on work and productivity, became a bestseller. It sparked conversations across industries and led to numerous speaking engagements and media appearances for Fried. Through these opportunities, he connected with influential figures in the business world, significantly expanding his professional network.

Jason Fried's journey with "Rework" illustrates the power of a book in networking. By co-authoring this provocative book, Fried and his co-author David Heinemeier Hansson challenged traditional business wisdom and provided actionable insights based on their experiences at Basecamp. The book's success was not just due to its content but also to its ability to start conversations. At conferences, industry events, and online forums, "Rework" became a reference point for discussions about new ways of working. This visibility translated into a broader network for Fried, connecting him with other thought leaders, potential partners, and clients.

Invitations to Speak at Conferences and Seminars

Beyond the initial publication, a successful book can also generate revenue through ongoing sales and licensing opportunities. Authors also leverage their book's success to secure speaking engagements, consulting contracts, or other business ventures, creating additional revenue streams and expanding their professional opportunities.

Authors are often invited to speak at conferences and seminars, providing them with a platform to share their insights and connect with a broader audience. Speaking engagements can significantly enhance your visibility and reputation, allowing you to establish yourself as an expert in your field.

A book can bring you to the attention of a wider audience, including potential clients, collaborators, or even the media. It can lead to speaking engagements, interviews, and other opportunities for exposure. Increased visibility enhances your professional reputation and opens doors to new avenues of growth and recognition. Writing allows you to showcase your knowledge and expertise in a particular field. You can establish your credibility by sharing your insights, experiences, and research findings within your domain. Your written works provide evidence of your depth of understanding and can contribute to building your reputation as a thought leader.

For example, when Rand Fishkin, co-founder of Moz, published "Lost and Founder," he was already a well-known figure in the SEO community. However, the book's publication opened up new speaking opportunities at conferences that were not solely focused on SEO but encompassed broader themes of entrepreneurship and startup culture. Fishkin's book provided a new dimension to his professional persona, making him a sought-after speaker at various industry events. These engagements allowed him to network with a diverse range of professionals and expand his influence beyond his initial niche.

Just like it worked out for Fishkin, publishing a book can also help enhance your reputation within your industry. It positions you as a thought leader, someone who is actively contributing to the advancement of knowledge and innovation. This increased visibility can lead to better invitations for speaking engagements, consulting opportunities, and media exposure, further elevating your professional standing.

Collaborative Ventures

Books can also lead to collaborative ventures, including co-authoring projects, research partnerships, and business collaborations. When you publish a book, you demonstrate your expertise and thought leadership, making you an attractive partner for others in your field.

The process of publishing and promoting a book can help you expand your professional network. Engaging with readers, fellow experts, and industry professionals through book events, conferences, and online platforms can lead to valuable connections. These connections can result in partnerships, collaborations, and business opportunities that further enhance your career trajectory. Writing also allows you to connect with like-minded individuals, experts, and influencers in your field. Through collaborations, joint publications, and contributions to collective works, you can leverage your networks to amplify your reach, exchange ideas, and gain further credibility within your communities.

An excellent example of this is the collaboration between Reid Hoffman and Chris Yeh on "Blitzscaling." Hoffman, co-founder of LinkedIn, and Yeh, an entrepreneur and investor, teamed up to write about the strategy of blitzscaling, which focuses on growing companies at a breakneck pace. Their collaboration brought together two distinct perspectives, enriching the content of the book and broadening its appeal. This partnership also expanded their networks, as they combined their individual connections and reached out to a more extensive audience through joint speaking engagements and promotional activities.

Another example is the collaboration between Brad Feld and Jason Mendelson, who co-authored "Venture Deals: Be Smarter Than Your Lawyer and Venture Capitalist." Feld and Mendelson, both venture capitalists with extensive experience, combined their knowledge to create a comprehensive guide on venture capital deals. This book not only solidified their authority in the venture capital space but also led to numerous collaborative opportunities, including workshops, webinars, and consulting engagements. Their joint efforts enhanced their visibility and credibility, attracting a broader network of entrepreneurs, investors, and industry professionals.

Increasing Referrals and Recommendations

A book can increase your referrals and recommendations by establishing you as a credible and authoritative figure. When people read your book and find value in your insights, they are more likely to recommend you to others within their network. This organic growth of your network can lead to new business opportunities, partnerships, and collaborations.

"The only way to achieve success is through hard work. So, don't be afraid to roll up your sleeves and put in the effort."

Case Study: Tim Ferriss and "The 4-Hour Workweek"

Tim Ferriss, author of "The 4-Hour Workweek," experienced a significant boost in referrals and recommendations following the publication of his book. Before the book, Ferriss was a relatively unknown entrepreneur.

However, "The 4-Hour Workweek" quickly became a bestseller, and its unconventional approach to productivity and lifestyle design resonated with a wide audience. As readers implemented Ferriss's strategies and saw results, they began to recommend his book to their friends, colleagues, and clients. This word-of-mouth promotion expanded Ferriss's network, leading to new business opportunities, partnerships, and a strong personal brand.

Ferriss's book also led to numerous speaking engagements, media appearances, and consulting opportunities. As more people discovered the value in his insights, his reputation grew, and so did his professional network. This expansion was not limited to the business world; Ferriss also connected with influencers in the health, fitness, and lifestyle sectors, further broadening his reach and influence.

Media and PR Opportunities

You may have noticed some people in your field getting a lot more attention than you just because they are published authors. Even if your knowledge stacks up better when compared to theirs, they will be chosen over you because they have the added title of being 'a bestselling author' to their identity. Therefore, for better visibility in your field and in seeking media coverage, being an authority and an expert is vital, and one of the best ways of being an authority is to author a book about your topic. Once you have a book under your belt, getting media coverage becomes ten times easier. And this is not the case just for the media.

In 2022, it was estimated that only a very small percentage of founders and thought leaders had authored books, potentially less than 1% or even

0.5%. However, many of those who did write books enjoyed a disproportionate amount of influence and opportunities. They often leveraged their authorship to enhance their personal brands, establish themselves as thought leaders in their respective industries, and gain speaking engagements and media exposure. Let us call them "The Top 1%".

Writing a book can attract significant media attention, leading to interviews, features, and guest appearances on various platforms. Media coverage can amplify your message and increase your visibility, connecting you with a broader audience and expanding your network.

> **Sheryl Sandberg and "Lean In"**
>
> Sheryl Sandberg, COO of Facebook, authored "Lean In: Women, Work, and the Will to Lead," which became a significant catalyst for discussions on gender equality in the workplace. Sandberg's book provided a platform for her to share her experiences and advocate for women's empowerment. "Lean In" sparked a global movement, leading to the creation of Lean In Circles—peer groups that meet regularly to support each other and learn new skills.
>
> The success of "Lean In" significantly expanded Sandberg's professional network. She was invited to speak at numerous conferences, including TED and the World Economic Forum, where she connected with other influential leaders and advocates. Her book also led to collaborations with organizations such as the Lean In Foundation, which supports initiatives aimed at closing the gender leadership gap. Through her book, Sandberg not only expanded her network but also created a lasting impact on the conversation around gender equality in the workplace.

A book increases your credibility, and being credible is important if you are a growing business. It is also a PR opportunity. Let us say your startup has come up with a fascinating new invention. As the CEO of your company, you have written about your journey of invention. The book gives a detailed look into who you are. It describes your invention and explains how it is going to help people. How exactly is it a PR opportunity?

Well, tech news platforms and magazines are always on the lookout for new content. Once your book hits the market, your PR agent can pitch your book to these platforms. Since it is an innovative invention, along with a book on the same, you will be written about on these platforms. Having written about on news platforms increases your popularity and adds to your credibility. Every coverage that you get is valuable. Thanks to this, your book will become an interview resource for all your future stories, furthering your popularity. You will be invited to talk shows and podcasts.

Case Study: Malcolm Gladwell and "The Tipping Point"

Malcolm Gladwell, a journalist and author, published "The Tipping Point: How Little Things Can Make a Big Difference," which examines how small actions can create a tipping point, leading to significant changes. The book's success garnered widespread media attention, with Gladwell being interviewed by major media outlets such as The New York Times, NPR, and CNN. This media exposure not only boosted book sales but also expanded Gladwell's professional network.

Through his media appearances, Gladwell connected with other thought leaders, policymakers, and business executives, leading to new opportunities for speaking engagements, consulting work, and collaborative projects. The media coverage of "The Tipping Point" also helped Gladwell establish himself as a prominent voice in the field of social psychology and business, further expanding his influence and network.

Research and Citations

Research supports the idea that authorship can enhance networking opportunities. A study published in the Journal of Management Development found that thought leadership, demonstrated through authored content such as books, significantly increases an individual's perceived expertise and credibility. This increased credibility makes others more likely to seek out their insights and collaborate with them on projects.

Additionally, the Pew Research Center found that individuals who publish books are more likely to be invited to speak at industry events and conferences. This exposure further enhances their visibility and connects them with a broader network of professionals.

According to a survey conducted by BookBaby, 83% of business leaders who have written a book reported a significant positive impact on their careers. This impact includes increased networking opportunities, more invitations to speak at events, and a higher likelihood of being sought after for collaborations and partnerships.

Writing a book can significantly expand your professional network. It serves as a powerful tool for establishing new connections, enhancing your visibility, and opening up opportunities for collaboration. As you embark on your authorship journey, remember that your book is not just a repository of knowledge but a bridge that connects you to a broader community of professionals, partners, and potential collaborators. By leveraging the power of your book, you can create meaningful relationships, drive your career forward, and make a lasting impact in your industry.

> *"Opportunities do not float like clouds in the sky. They are attached to people. If you're looking for an opportunity, you're really looking for a person."*
> **— Reid Hoffman (Co-founder, LinkedIn)**

> "The richest people in the world look for and build networks; everyone else looks for work."
> — **Robert Kiyosaki**

Key Takeaways

- **Authorship as a Networking Tool**: Writing a book provides a tangible representation of your expertise and serves as a powerful conversation starter, opening doors to new professional connections.

- **Speaking Engagements**: Authors are often invited to speak at conferences and seminars, enhancing their visibility and reputation while providing opportunities to connect with a broader audience.

- **Collaborative Ventures**: A book can lead to collaborative projects, including co-authoring, research partnerships, and business collaborations, by demonstrating your expertise and thought leadership.

- **Referrals and Recommendations**: A well-received book can increase your referrals and recommendations, as readers who find value in your insights are likely to share them with others.

- **Media and PR Opportunities**: Writing a book can attract significant media attention, leading to interviews, features, and guest appearances on various platforms, further expanding your network.

4

ENHANCING STAKEHOLDER RELATIONSHIPS

"Effective communication helps to build relationships, foster trust, and ensure that everyone is aligned and working towards common goals."

—**Indra Nooyi**

In the high-stakes environment of startups, fostering robust relationships with stakeholders is crucial. Whether it's investors, clients, or team members, maintaining clear and effective communication can be the difference between success and failure.

Imagine you've just finished a presentation to potential investors. Instead of leaving them with just a business card, you hand over a copy of your newly published book. This gesture alone speaks volumes about your commitment to transparency and thought leadership. Immediately, you've given them a resource that showcases your expertise and vision.

This scenario is not far-fetched; many startup founders have used their books to build and enhance relationships with their stakeholders.

Improving Communication

A book can serve as an invaluable tool for improving communication with stakeholders. It provides a comprehensive medium through which you can convey your vision, address common concerns, and answer frequently asked questions in a detailed and thoughtful manner.

The process of translating thoughts into words requires authors to distill complex ideas into clear and coherent language. This practice sharpens your ability to convey intricate concepts in a manner that is comprehensible to a diverse readership. Authors refine their communication through meticulous editing and rewriting, enhancing their capacity to articulate even the most intricate notions.

Crafting a book necessitates understanding the reader's vantage point. Authors embark on a journey of empathy, anticipating the questions and concerns that readers might have. This process trains authors to tailor their messaging to resonate with varied audiences, fostering a heightened sensitivity to different perspectives.

The collaborative writing process involves engaging with editors, peer reviewers, and early readers. Authors learn to embrace feedback as a tool for growth, allowing them to assess their work and make necessary improvements critically. This interaction hones the skill of integrating diverse viewpoints while maintaining the coherence of their narrative.

Consider the example of Blake Mycoskie, founder of TOMS and author of "Start Something That Matters." In his book, Mycoskie shares the story behind TOMS' one-for-one business model and the company's commitment to social responsibility. By articulating the mission and values of TOMS in a personal and engaging way, Mycoskie has effectively communicated with a broad audience of stakeholders, including customers, investors, and employees. His book has become a powerful tool for conveying the company's ethos and fostering a deeper connection with stakeholders.

The culmination of writing a book is not just a finish line; it's an amalgamation of effort and dedication woven over time. Completing and publishing a book generates a sense of accomplishment that reverberates through an author's sense of self. This triumph bolsters self-confidence, affirming that the author's dedication and expertise are valued.

As readers engage with the book's content and peers acknowledge the insights shared, authors receive validation of their expertise. The recognition from the audience and industry leaders alike amplifies their self-assuredness in their domain knowledge, further emboldening them to present their ideas with conviction.

By addressing common questions and interests in your book, you can provide stakeholders with a clear understanding of your business model, goals, and strategies. This transparency helps build trust and confidence in your leadership.

Addressing Common Questions and Interests

A well-written book can serve as an extended FAQ for your business, addressing common questions and concerns that stakeholders may have. By providing detailed explanations and insights, you can preemptively answer many of the questions that investors, clients, or partners might pose.

Case Study: Elon Musk and "Tesla, SpaceX, and the Quest for a Fantastic Future"

While Elon Musk didn't write "Tesla, SpaceX, and the Quest for a Fantastic Future" himself, the biography by Ashlee Vance serves a similar purpose. The book provides an in-depth look at Musk's ventures, shedding light on his vision, challenges, and successes. For potential investors and partners, this book offers valuable insights into Musk's mindset and the future of his companies. It helps answer many questions about the rationale behind his ambitious projects and his approach to business, thereby enhancing communication and understanding with stakeholders.

In your book, consider including sections that address the most common queries you receive. For example, if you often get questions about your startup's sustainability practices, dedicate a chapter to explaining your initiatives and the impact they have. This proactive approach not only educates stakeholders but also demonstrates your commitment to transparency and accountability.

Building Trust and Loyalty

Trust is a cornerstone of any successful relationship, particularly in the startup world where uncertainty and risk are ever-present. A book can play a significant role in building trust and loyalty among your stakeholders by demonstrating your expertise, transparency, and dedication.

Though writing and editing a book require a fair amount of time and research, it can have transformative results for your business. As you use your book to bolster your credibility and expand your market reach, you will be able to grow at a much faster rate than ever before. By writing a book, entrepreneurs can build their personal brand, establish their expertise, and build trust with potential clients.

Example: Howard Schultz and "Onward"

Howard Schultz, the CEO of Starbucks, authored "Onward: How Starbucks Fought for Its Life without Losing Its Soul," a book that chronicles the company's turnaround during the 2008 financial crisis. Schultz's candid narrative about the challenges and decisions faced during this tumultuous period provided stakeholders with an inside look at the company's strategy and the values that guided its recovery. This transparency reinforced trust among investors, employees, and customers, highlighting Schultz's commitment to preserving the integrity of the Starbucks brand while navigating through adversity.

Demonstrating Commitment to Transparency and Leadership

Writing a book requires a significant investment of time and effort, which clearly demonstrates your commitment to your business and your stakeholders. By sharing your journey, challenges, and successes in a detailed and authentic manner, you convey a message of transparency and leadership.

As mentioned earlier, a book serves as a powerful tool for personal branding and establishing authority in your field. By sharing your expertise, insights, and experiences in a well-crafted book, you solidify your position as an industry expert. It becomes a testament to your thoughts and ideas, showcasing your unique perspective and knowledge.

Moreover, a well-written book can capture the attention of peers, colleagues, and potential clients, creating valuable connections and fostering professional relationships.

Publishing a book can enhance your reputation within your industry, positioning you as a thought leader who actively contributes to the advancement of knowledge and innovation. This increased visibility can lead to invitations for speaking engagements, consulting opportunities, and media exposure, further elevating your professional standing.

A book is a legacy piece that preserves your knowledge and insights for future generations. It becomes a valuable resource that can impact and inspire others long after its publication. By capturing your ideas in a book, you leave a lasting imprint on your industry and contribute to the collective knowledge of your field.

Case Study: Patty McCord and "Powerful"

Patty McCord, former Chief Talent Officer at Netflix, authored "Powerful: Building a Culture of Freedom and Responsibility," where she shared her experiences and insights on creating a high-performing workplace culture. McCord's book outlines the principles that shaped Netflix's innovative HR practices, providing stakeholders with a clear understanding of the company's approach to talent management. By openly discussing the successes  and failures of these practices, McCord has demonstrated a commitment to transparency and continuous improvement, building trust with current and potential stakeholders.

"Powerful" cemented McCord's position in the industry while securing her legacy for generations to come by publishing a record of her work.

Enhancing Relationships with Investors

Investors are critical stakeholders in any startup, and building strong relationships with them can be pivotal to your success. A book can serve as a valuable tool for engaging with investors, providing them with deeper insights into your business and vision.

Example: Ben Horowitz and "The Hard Thing About Hard Things"

Ben Horowitz, co-founder of Andreessen Horowitz, authored "The Hard Thing About Hard Things," a book that offers candid advice on the challenges of building and running a startup. By sharing his personal experiences and the difficult decisions he had to make, Horowitz provides investors with a realistic view of the entrepreneurial journey. His transparency and honesty help build trust and credibility, fostering stronger relationships with investors who appreciate his forthrightness and expertise.

Enhancing Relationships with Clients

Clients are another crucial group of stakeholders whose trust and loyalty are essential for the growth of your business. A book can help you build stronger relationships with clients by showcasing your expertise, addressing their concerns, and providing valuable insights.

Example: Jay Baer and "Hug Your Haters"

Jay Baer, a renowned marketing consultant, authored "Hug Your Haters: How to Embrace Complaints and Keep Your Customers," a book that explores the importance of customer service and how businesses can turn negative feedback into positive outcomes. Baer's book provides actionable strategies for improving customer relations, demonstrating his expertise and commitment to helping businesses succeed. By addressing common client concerns and offering practical solutions, Baer builds trust and credibility with his clients, enhancing their loyalty and satisfaction.

Enhancing Relationships with Employees

Employees are the backbone of any startup, and fostering strong relationships with them is vital for creating a positive and productive work environment. A book can help you connect with your employees on a deeper level by sharing your vision, values, and leadership philosophy.

Example: Tony Hsieh and "Delivering Happiness"

Tony Hsieh, the late CEO of Zappos, authored "Delivering Happiness: A Path to Profits, Passion, and Purpose," a book that outlines his philosophy on company culture and customer service. Hsieh's book provides employees with a clear understanding of the values and principles that guide Zappos, fostering a sense of purpose and belonging. By sharing his personal journey and the lessons he learned along the way, Hsieh built trust and loyalty among his employees, creating a strong and cohesive company culture.

Building Relationships with the Wider Community

In addition to internal stakeholders, a book can help you build relationships with the broader community, including industry peers, potential partners, and the public. By sharing your knowledge and experiences, you can establish yourself as a thought leader and contribute to the growth and development of your industry.

Example: Jessica Jackley and "Clay Water Brick"

Jessica Jackley, co-founder of Kiva, authored "Clay Water Brick: Finding Inspiration from Entrepreneurs Who Do the Most with the Least," a book that tells the stories of entrepreneurs from around the world who have overcome significant challenges to achieve success. Jackley's book highlights the importance of social entrepreneurship and the impact it can have on communities. By sharing these inspiring stories, Jackley has built relationships with a global audience of entrepreneurs, investors, and supporters who are passionate about making a difference.

Numerous studies and expert opinions support the benefits of writing a book for enhancing stakeholder relationships. According to a study published in the Journal of Business Communication, transparent communication is a key factor in building trust and loyalty among stakeholders. The study found that stakeholders are more likely to trust and support leaders who openly share their vision, goals, and challenges.

Furthermore, a report by the Public Relations Society of America (PRSA) highlights the importance of thought leadership in fostering strong stakeholder relationships. The report states that thought leadership, demonstrated through authored content such as books, significantly enhances credibility and trust, leading to stronger and more productive relationships with stakeholders.

Therefore, writing a book can significantly enhance your relationships with various stakeholders. It serves as a powerful tool for improving communication, building trust and loyalty, and fostering strong connections with investors, clients, employees, and the wider community. By sharing your knowledge and experiences, you can create meaningful relationships, drive your business forward, and make a lasting impact in your industry.

> *"The most important thing in communication is hearing what isn't said."*
> — **Peter Drucker**

Key Takeaways

- **Improving Communication:** A book serves as a comprehensive medium for conveying your vision, addressing common concerns, and answering frequently asked questions, thereby improving communication with stakeholders.

- **Building Trust and Loyalty:** By demonstrating your expertise, transparency, and dedication through your book, you can build trust and loyalty among investors, clients, employees, and the wider community.

- **Enhancing Relationships with Investors and Clients:** A book provides investors with deeper insights into your business and vision, fostering stronger relationships based on trust and credibility. It also showcases your expertise and addressing client concerns in your book can help build trust and loyalty among your clients, enhancing their satisfaction and engagement.

- **Enhancing Relationships with Employees:** Sharing your vision, values, and leadership philosophy in your book can help connect with your employees on a deeper level, fostering a positive and productive work environment.

- **Building Relationships with the Wider Community:** A book can help you establish yourself as a thought leader and build relationships with industry peers, potential partners, and the public, contributing to the growth and development of your industry.

5

BOOSTING YOUR BRAND'S REPUTATION

"A book is the greatest weapon in a marketer's arsenal. It can establish you as a thought leader and differentiate your startup in a crowded market."
—**Guy Kawasaki, The Art of the Start**

In the hyper-competitive world of startups, reputation can be a crucial differentiator. Imagine launching a new product, and instead of the typical marketing campaign, your announcement includes a book that delves into the story behind your brand, the innovation process, and your vision for the future. The book garners media attention attracting a broad readership and positions your brand as a thought leader in the industry. This scenario illustrates the power of a book in boosting your brand's reputation. Many startup founders have leveraged their authorship to elevate their company's brand and credibility in the marketplace.

Marketing and Branding

Unlike traditional marketing materials, a book offers a unique and compelling way to communicate your brand's story and values. It provides depth and context, fostering a more personal and meaningful engagement with your audience, making it a cornerstone of your marketing strategy.

Publishing a book is one of the best ways of getting attention and gaining trust; it is a multipurpose marketing tool. Your book can help you with almost anything you want: sales, media publicity, word-of-mouth publicity, recognition as an authority, etc. The act of writing and publishing a book is not just a marketing strategy, it's a powerful tool that can empower you to achieve your goals and establish your authority in your field.

Consider the example of Phil Knight, co-founder of Nike, and his memoir "Shoe Dog." Knight's book offers an insider's perspective on the history of Nike, from its humble beginnings to becoming a global powerhouse. By sharing his entrepreneurial journey, Knight has effectively used the book to reinforce Nike's brand values of innovation, resilience, and excellence. "Shoe Dog" not only resonated with consumers but also attracted media attention, generating positive publicity for Nike.

Leveraging Your Book for Startup's Growth and Brand Building

A book can serve as a powerful tool for startup growth and brand building. By sharing your expertise and vision, you can attract new customers, partners, and investors who align with your values and mission.

Particularly, a book that garners commendation can be a fulcrum of transformation in your professional sphere. It can sway the scales in your favor by garnering interested investors' attention and opening doors to new collaborations with other industry experts. And, in some cases, heralding a transition into realms like consulting, teaching, or dedicating oneself to full-time writing. A book's impact goes beyond just its content, often sculpting new trajectories.

Beyond the contours of book sales, an author's creation can blossom into diversified income streams. Related merchandise, online courses, workshops, and even speaking engagements emerge as extensions of the book's themes. This realm of supplementary revenue not only adds a financial dimension but extends the influence and impact of the author's work.

As the book reaches readers across the globe, it forges a nexus between the author and an expansive audience. The ideas, insights, and perspectives encapsulated within the pages ripple outward, influencing not only individual readers but also industry trends and the broader discourse. The author's reach becomes global, and their influence transcends boundaries.

The journey of writing a book isn't confined to the act of creation; it is a potent catalyst for professional transformation. The book acts as an ambassador, attesting to an author's expertise, shaping their brand, fostering connections, opening avenues for public speaking, sculpting career trajectories, generating diverse income streams, and broadening their sphere of influence. In embracing the author's identity, the book becomes a lodestar of professional advancement.

Consider the example of Eric Ries and his book, "The Lean Startup."

Eric Ries, the author of "The Lean Startup," not only established himself as a thought leader but also significantly boosted the reputation of his consulting business. The lean startup methodology introduced in the book became a foundational principle for many new and existing businesses. Ries leveraged the success of his book to build a consulting firm that helps startups implement lean methodologies. The book's influence has led to numerous speaking engagements, workshops, and advisory roles, all of which have contributed to the growth and reputation of his business.

Media and PR Opportunities

Establishing yourself as an authority figure or thought leader, with your book, enhances your credibility. This credibility then attracts media attention, as journalists often look for authoritative voices to feature in their stories. By being featured in interviews and articles, you have the opportunity to share your brand's vision, goals, and innovations with a broader audience.

As mentioned earlier, books can generate significant media and PR opportunities, providing you with a platform to share your story and insights with a wider range of audiences.

But media coverage can also amplify your message and enhance your startup's visibility, attracting potential customers, investors, and partners alike.

Example: Sheryl Sandberg and "Lean In"

Sheryl Sandberg's book "Lean In: Women, Work, and the Will to Lead" sparked a global conversation about gender equality in the workplace. The book's success led to extensive media coverage, with Sandberg appearing on major news networks, talk shows, and prominent publications. This media attention not only boosted Sandberg's personal brand but also highlighted Facebook's commitment to diversity and inclusion. The positive publicity generated by the book helped to enhance Facebook's reputation as a progressive and socially responsible company.

Becoming a Go-To Expert for Interviews and Articles

Publishing a book positions you as an expert in your field, making you a go-to source for interviews and articles. Journalists and media outlets frequently seek out authors for their insights and expertise, providing you with additional opportunities to promote your brand or business and its mission.

Moreover, being recognized as an expert can open doors to various speaking engagements, panels, and conferences, further solidifying your position as a leader in your field. These opportunities allow you to network with other industry leaders, potential investors, and partners, fostering relationships that can be beneficial for your business's growth.

Media coverage and interviews can drive traffic to your brand's website and social media platforms, increasing awareness and engagement with your brand. Potential customers, clients, and collaborators are more likely to trust and support a brand led by someone recognized for their expertise and thought leadership.

Example: Gary Vaynerchuk and "Crush It!"

Gary Vaynerchuk, a serial entrepreneur and social media expert, authored "Crush It! Why NOW Is the Time to Cash In on Your Passion." The book's success positioned Vaynerchuk as a leading authority on digital marketing and personal branding. As a result, he has become a sought-after speaker and media personality, regularly appearing on major news outlets and industry podcasts. These opportunities have allowed Vaynerchuk to promote his businesses, VaynerMedia and VaynerX, enhancing their reputation and attracting new clients.

Using Your Book to Drive Content Marketing

A book can provide a wealth of content for your marketing efforts, from blog posts and social media updates to webinars and podcasts. By repurposing the content from your book, you can create a consistent and compelling narrative that reinforces your brand message across multiple channels.

Leveraging your book for content marketing allows you to extract valuable insights, stories, and lessons to share with your audience. Each chapter or section of your book can be transformed into a series of blog posts, offering in-depth explorations of specific topics. These posts can drive traffic to your website, improve SEO, and establish you and your brand as a reliable source of industry knowledge.

Your book's content can also be adapted for social media updates, providing bite-sized, shareable nuggets of information that engage your audience and encourage interaction. By regularly posting quotes, tips, and excerpts from your book, you can maintain a steady stream of content that keeps your followers informed and interested.

Webinars and podcasts are another effective way to repurpose your book's content. Hosting a webinar series based on your book's themes allows you to delve deeper into subjects and engage with your audience in real-time, answering questions and fostering a sense of community. Similarly, discussing your book's topics on a podcast can reach a wider audience, offering them valuable insights while promoting your book and business organization.

As per Forbes[1], creating downloadable resources such as whitepapers, infographics, and e-books based on your book can serve as lead magnets, attracting potential customers and clients to your website. These resources can provide added value to your audience while capturing their contact information for future marketing efforts.

Repurposing your book's content across various platforms ensures that your message remains consistent and reinforces your brand's narrative. It maximizes

---

1. Forbes:https://www.forbes.com/sites/theyec/2023/03/07/how-to-use-e-books-and-white-papers-as-lead-magnets-for-your-marketing-campaigns/

the return on investment from your book by extending its reach and impact, positioning your brand as a thought leader in your industry.

Using your book to drive content marketing not only amplifies your brand message but also provides a diverse array of materials to engage with your audience. It enables you to maintain a cohesive and compelling presence across multiple channels, ultimately contributing to your brand's growth and success.

Example: Neil Patel and "Hustle"

Neil Patel, a digital marketing expert and co-author of "Hustle: The Power to Charge Your Life with Money, Meaning, and Momentum," uses content from his book to fuel his content marketing strategy. Patel frequently shares insights and excerpts from "Hustle" on his blog, social media platforms, and podcasts. This approach has helped him maintain a consistent brand message, attract a loyal following, and enhance the reputation of his digital marketing agencies, Neil Patel Digital and NP Accel.

Establishing Thought Leadership

A book can establish you as a thought leader in your industry, showcasing your expertise and insights. Thought leadership can enhance your startup's reputation, making it easier to attract top talent, secure partnerships, and gain customer trust.

Books have a lasting impact, remaining relevant long after their publication. By documenting your vision and expertise, you create a permanent resource that can continue to influence and inspire others.

When you publish a book, you create a timeless asset that preserves your ideas, strategies, and insights for future generations. This enduring relevance ensures that your contributions to your industry can continue to shape thinking and practices long after the book's initial release. Your book serves as a reference point for current and future professionals, providing them with valuable knowledge and inspiration.

The long-term impact of a book extends to your personal and professional legacy. By capturing your expertise in a written form, you leave a lasting imprint on your field, solidifying your position as a thought leader and innovator. This documented expertise can influence industry standards, guide emerging trends, and inspire the next wave of entrepreneurs and professionals.

Moreover, a book can become a cornerstone of your brand's intellectual property, contributing to its long-term value. As new stakeholders, whether they are employees, partners, or customers, come into contact with your book, they gain insight into the foundational principles and visionary thinking that drive your organization. This ongoing engagement with your ideas helps to sustain and grow your influence over time.

Books also have the unique ability to reach a wide and diverse audience. Unlike transient forms of content, such as social media posts or articles, a book can be discovered and appreciated by new readers years after its publication. This longevity enhances its potential to impact a broader range of individuals, spreading your message and vision across different contexts and time periods.

In educational settings, your book can be used as a teaching tool, further extending its impact. Universities, training programs, and professional development courses may adopt your book as a core text, ensuring that your expertise contributes to the education and development of future leaders in your industry.

Creating a book establishes a long-term impact that endures well beyond its publication date. It documents your vision and expertise, providing a permanent resource that can continue to influence and inspire others. By capturing your insights in a lasting format, you ensure that your contributions remain relevant and impactful, enhancing your legacy and sustaining your influence in your industry.

Example: Clayton Christensen and "The Innovator's Dilemma"

Clayton Christensen, a professor at Harvard Business School, authored "The Innovator's Dilemma," a groundbreaking book that introduced the concept of disruptive innovation. Christensen's insights have had a profound impact on the business world, influencing how companies approach innovation and growth. His book established him as a leading authority on innovation, and his work has been cited by numerous CEOs, entrepreneurs, and academics.

The success of "The Innovator's Dilemma" has not only boosted Christensen's personal reputation but also enhanced the prestige of Harvard Business School.

Creating Long-Term Impact

Books have a lasting impact, remaining relevant long after their publication. By documenting your vision and expertise, you create a permanent resource that can continue to influence and inspire others.

Example: Jim Collins and "Good to Great"

Jim Collins, a management consultant and author, wrote "Good to Great: Why Some Companies Make the Leap...and Others Don't," which explores the factors that enable companies to achieve enduring success. The book has become a classic in the field of business management, continuously referenced by leaders and educators. Collins's insights have had a long-term impact on how businesses approach strategy and leadership, cementing his reputation as a thought leader. "Good to Great" has helped countless companies improve their performance and achieve sustainable growth.

Enhancing Your Startup's Story

A book allows you to tell your startup's story in a compelling and detailed manner, providing context and depth that other marketing materials might lack. By sharing the journey of your startup, including the challenges and triumphs, you can create a narrative that resonates with your audience and strengthens your brand.

Example: Blake Mycoskie and "Start Something That Matters"

Blake Mycoskie, founder of TOMS, authored "Start Something That Matters," which tells the story of how he built TOMS on the principle of giving back. Mycoskie's book provides an in-depth look at the inspiration behind the one-for-one business model and the impact it has had on communities around the world. By sharing the journey of TOMS, Mycoskie has created a powerful narrative that resonates with customers, investors, and partners. The book has reinforced TOMS' brand as a socially responsible company and has inspired other entrepreneurs to incorporate social good into their business models.

Building Emotional Connections

A book can help you build emotional connections with your audience by sharing personal stories, insights, and experiences. These connections can enhance customer loyalty and create advocates for your brand.

Example: Howard Schultz and "Onward"

Howard Schultz, the former CEO of Starbucks, authored "Onward: How Starbucks Fought for Its Life without Losing Its Soul," a book that chronicles the company's turnaround during the 2008 financial crisis. Schultz's candid narrative about the challenges and decisions faced during this period provides readers with an inside look at the values and principles that guide Starbucks. By sharing his personal journey and the emotional highs and lows of leading Starbucks through adversity, Schultz has built strong emotional connections with readers. These connections have reinforced customer loyalty and strengthened the Starbucks brand.

Enhancing Employee Engagement

A book can also enhance employee engagement by providing a clear and compelling vision of your organisation's mission and values. Employees who understand and connect with the company's purpose are more likely to be motivated and committed to their work.

Example: Tony Hsieh and "Delivering Happiness"

Tony Hsieh, the late CEO of Zappos, authored "Delivering Happiness: A Path to Profits, Passion, and Purpose," which outlines his philosophy on company culture and customer service. Hsieh's book provides employees with a clear understanding of the values and principles that guide Zappos, fostering a sense of purpose and belonging. By sharing his personal journey and the lessons he learned along the way, Hsieh built trust and loyalty among his employees, creating a strong and cohesive company culture.

Building Relationships with Partners and Suppliers

A book can help you build relationships with partners and suppliers by showcasing your expertise and vision. By sharing your organisation's story and mission, you can attract partners and suppliers who align with your values and goals.

Example: Jessica Jackley and "Clay Water Brick"

Jessica Jackley, co-founder of Kiva, authored "Clay Water Brick: Finding Inspiration from Entrepreneurs Who Do the Most with the Least," a book that tells the stories of entrepreneurs from around the world who have overcome significant challenges to achieve success. Jackley's book highlights the importance of social entrepreneurship and the impact it can have on communities. By sharing these inspiring stories, Jackley has built relationships with a global audience of entrepreneurs, investors, and supporters who are passionate about making a difference. Her book has also attracted partners and suppliers who share Kiva's mission of providing microloans to underserved communities.

Strengthening Your Personal Brand

A book can also strengthen your personal brand, enhancing your reputation and visibility. By sharing your knowledge and experiences, you can establish yourself as a thought leader and attract new opportunities for growth and collaboration.

Example: Simon Sinek and "Start with Why"

Simon Sinek, a leadership expert, authored "Start with Why: How Great Leaders Inspire Everyone to Take Action," a book that explores the importance of understanding the purpose behind your work. Sinek's book has become a bestseller and has established him as a leading authority on leadership and motivation. Through his book, Sinek has strengthened his personal brand, attracting speaking engagements, consulting opportunities, and media appearances. His insights have resonated with leaders and organizations around the world, enhancing his reputation and influence.

Creating a Legacy

A book can create a lasting legacy, allowing you to share your knowledge and experiences with future generations. By documenting your journey and insights, you can leave a lasting impact on your industry and inspire others to follow in your footsteps.

Moreover, writing a book allows you to leave a lasting legacy that extends far beyond your immediate role within the organization. It becomes a testament to your contributions, a tangible embodiment of your knowledge, and a guidepost for future generations. Your book would serve as a beacon, illuminating the way for others and contributing to your industry's ongoing development and evolution.

Writing a book as a startup founder provides a remarkable opportunity to share your insights, influence your industry, enrich your personal growth, and leave a lasting legacy. It is a chance to contribute to the development of professionals and to make a meaningful impact that extends far beyond the confines of your immediate organization. Embrace the power of the written word and embark on this transformative journey that holds the potential to shape the future of your industry.

By putting your thoughts and experiences into writing you have the power to establish your credibility and influence. Whether you choose to express yourself through books, articles, blog posts, or other written mediums, you are given a remarkable opportunity to articulate your viewpoints, share your expertise, and contribute to the ongoing conversation within your field or areas of interest.

Example: Warren Buffett and "The Essays of Warren Buffett"

Warren Buffett, one of the most successful investors in history, has shared his wisdom through "The Essays of Warren Buffett: Lessons for Corporate America," a collection of his annual shareholder letters. These essays provide valuable insights into Buffett's investment philosophy and business principles. By compiling his thoughts and experiences in a book, Buffett has created a lasting legacy that continues to influence investors and business leaders. His book serves as a timeless resource for those seeking to learn from one of the greatest minds in the business world. Numerous studies and expert opinions support the benefits of writing a book for boosting your startup's reputation. According to a study published in the Journal of Business Research, thought leadership, demonstrated through authored content such as books, significantly enhances credibility and trust. This increased credibility can lead to greater visibility and reputation, attracting new customers, investors, and partners.

Furthermore, a report by the Public Relations Society of America (PRSA) highlights the importance of thought leadership in enhancing a company's reputation. The report states that thought leadership, demonstrated through authored content such as books, significantly enhances credibility and trust, leading to stronger and more productive relationships with stakeholders.

Writing a book can significantly boost your startup's reputation. It serves as a powerful tool for marketing and branding, attracting new opportunities for growth and collaboration and establishing you as a thought leader in your industry. By sharing your knowledge and experiences, you can create meaningful connections, drive your business forward, and make a lasting impact in your industry.

> *"It takes 20 years to build a reputation and five minutes to ruin it. If you think about that, you'll do things differently."*
> — **Warren Buffett**

Key Takeaways

- **Marketing and Branding:** A book can be a cornerstone of your marketing strategy, offering a unique and compelling way to communicate your brand's story and values.

- **Leveraging Your Book for Startup Growth:** By sharing your expertise and vision, you can attract new customers, partners, and investors who align with your values and mission.

- **Media and PR Opportunities:** Books can generate significant media and PR opportunities, providing you with a platform to share your story and insights with a broader audience.

- **Establishing Thought Leadership:** A book can establish you as a thought leader in your industry, showcasing your expertise and insights.

- **Creating Long-Term Impact:** Books have a lasting impact, remaining relevant long after their publication.

- **Building Emotional Connections:** A book can help you build emotional connections with your audience by sharing personal stories, insights, and experiences.

- **Enhancing Your Brand's Story:** A book allows you to tell your startup's story in a compelling and detailed manner, providing context and depth that other marketing materials might lack.

- **Enhancing Employee Engagement:** A book can enhance employee engagement by providing a clear and compelling vision of your startup's mission and values.

- **Building Relationships with Partners and Suppliers:** A book can help you build relationships with partners and suppliers by showcasing your expertise and vision.

- **Strengthening Your Personal Brand:** A book can strengthen your personal brand, enhancing your reputation and visibility.

- **Creating a Legacy:** A book can create a lasting legacy, allowing you to share your knowledge and experiences with future generations.

[YouTube Link](#)

6

PERSONAL AND PROFESSIONAL FULFILLMENT

"Each of us is a book waiting to be written, and that book, if written, results in a person explained."
—**Thomas M. Cirignano**

Imagine crossing the finish line of a marathon, the culmination of months of grueling training, discipline, and perseverance. As you hold up your finisher's medal, you feel a profound sense of accomplishment and fulfillment. Now, envision that instead of a medal, you're holding your published book—the result of years of experience, hard work, and dedication.

The pride and satisfaction of seeing your name on the cover of a book, sharing your insights with the world, can be incredibly fulfilling.

Writing a book is not just a professional milestone; it's a deeply personal achievement that can bring immense personal and professional fulfillment.

Achieving Personal Milestones

Writing a book is a significant personal milestone. It's a tangible manifestation of your expertise, experiences, and dedication. Completing a book requires discipline, focus, and a deep commitment to your subject matter. The journey from the initial idea to the final publication is often long and challenging, but the sense of accomplishment upon holding your book in your hands is unparalleled.

Writing a book is a journey of growth and self-discovery. Focusing on the joy of the writing process and thinking about the impact that your book can make, while being able to share your knowledge and experiences, is a highly satisfying feat. Just think about it, someone out there is quite clueless about something professionally or even personally, and your book is the clarity they need to get out of that slump. How fulfilling is that?

The Personal Satisfaction of Becoming a Published Author

The process of writing a book is a fiercely transformative journey. It pushes you to reflect deeply on your experiences, articulate your insights, and communicate your vision in a coherent and compelling way. This introspective process can be incredibly rewarding, as it allows you to gain a deeper understanding of your own knowledge and expertise.

For many authors, the satisfaction of becoming a published author is akin to completing a marathon. It's a testament to your perseverance, dedication, and hard work. This personal achievement can boost your self-esteem and confidence, reinforcing your belief in your abilities and potential.

Example: Scott Harrison and "Thirst"

Scott Harrison, founder of charity: water, authored "Thirst: A Story of Redemption, Compassion, and a Mission to Bring Clean Water to the World." Harrison's book chronicles his journey from a nightclub promoter to a social entrepreneur committed to solving the global water crisis. The personal satisfaction Harrison derived from sharing his story and mission through his book is evident. "Thirst" not only became a bestseller but also raised significant awareness and funds for charity: water, showcasing the profound personal and professional fulfillment that comes from becoming a published author.

Sharing Your Journey and Experiences

Writing a book gives you the opportunity to share your journey and experiences with a broader audience. Your story can inspire, educate, and empower others, creating a lasting impact on their lives. By sharing the lessons you've learned and the challenges you've overcome, you can provide valuable insights and guidance to others who are on similar paths.

The Impact of Sharing Your Story

Sharing your story can have a profound impact on your readers. It can provide them with inspiration, hope, and practical advice. Your book can serve as a roadmap for others, helping them navigate their own challenges and achieve their goals. This sense of contribution and the positive feedback you receive from readers can be deeply fulfilling.

Example: Sophia Amoruso and "#GIRLBOSS"

Sophia Amoruso, founder of Nasty Gal, authored "#GIRLBOSS," a book that chronicles her journey from starting an eBay store to building a multimillion-dollar fashion empire. Amoruso's candid and relatable storytelling resonated with a wide audience, particularly young women aspiring to break into the fashion industry. By sharing her journey and the lessons she learned along the way, Amoruso provided valuable insights and inspiration to her readers.  The success of "#GIRLBOSS" not only boosted Amoruso's personal brand but also created a movement, empowering countless women to pursue their dreams and build their own businesses.

Leaving a Legacy

Some authors may say, "I don't care about goals... I just want to write a book for myself or my family." This is an absolutely valid argument. People inevitably undergo struggles, and some want to document their journey, and the lessons learned in a book. They want their readers to discover the nuggets of wisdom they have unearthed during their journey, lay out advice that no one was around to give them. There could not be a more reasonable and noble goal to write a book. We, at Stardom Books, have worked with a billionaire who documented his journey in the form of a book for this very reason. Some senior experts also write a 'memoir' of their life story, with a number of personal stories, life lessons, anecdotes, and opinions.

A book can serve as a lasting legacy, preserving your knowledge and experiences for future generations. By documenting your journey and insights, you create a permanent record that can continue to inspire and educate others long after you're gone.

Creating a Lasting Impact in Your Field

Writing a book allows you to contribute to the body of knowledge in your field. Your insights and experiences can provide valuable contributions to the ongoing discourse in your industry. By sharing your expertise, you can help shape the future of your field and leave a lasting impact.

Writing a book also allows you to leave a lasting legacy that extends far beyond your immediate role within your organisation. It becomes a testament to your contributions, a tangible embodiment of your knowledge, and a guidepost for future generations. Your book would serve as a beacon, illuminating the way for others and contributing to your industry's ongoing development and evolution.

Writing a book as an entrepreneur provides a remarkable opportunity to share your insights, influence your industry, enrich your personal growth, and leave a lasting legacy. It is a chance to contribute to the development of professionals and to make a meaningful impact that extends far beyond the confines of your immediate organization.

Example: Clayton Christensen and "The Innovator's Dilemma"

Clayton Christensen, a professor at Harvard Business School, authored "The Innovator's Dilemma," a groundbreaking book that introduced the concept of disruptive innovation. Christensen's insights have had a profound impact on the business world, influencing how companies approach innovation and growth. His book has become a classic in the field of business management, continuously referenced by leaders and educators. Christensen's work has left a lasting legacy, shaping the discourse on innovation and guiding countless companies in their strategic decisions.

Contributing to Entrepreneurial Literature and Education

To start the journey of writing a book is to set out on a transformative adventure. It is an invitation to explore the depths of one's creativity, to delve into the realms of imagination, and to connect with readers on a profound level. By embracing the time, dedication, and perseverance required, aspiring authors can join the ranks of those who have left an indelible mark on literature and the world at large.

Your book can contribute to the broader entrepreneurial literature, providing valuable resources for aspiring entrepreneurs, educators, and researchers. By sharing your knowledge and experiences, you can help educate the next generation of entrepreneurs and contribute to the growth and development of the entrepreneurial ecosystem.

Example: Peter Thiel and "Zero to One"

Peter Thiel, co-founder of PayPal and Palantir Technologies, authored "Zero to One: Notes on Startups, or How to Build the Future." Thiel's book provides a unique perspective on innovation and entrepreneurship, offering insights on how to create and scale successful startups. "Zero to One" has become a must-read for entrepreneurs and has been incorporated into business school curricula around the world. Thiel's contributions to entrepreneurial literature and education have had a lasting impact, providing valuable guidance and inspiration to countless aspiring entrepreneurs.

Personal and Professional Growth

As illustrated in the examples above, these books, more than parchment and ink, have been conduits for personal growth, amplifying the influence of these thought leaders. They have chiseled personal brands that transcend boardrooms, fostering discussions, and catalyzing change. The pages of their books unfold stories of innovation, resilience, and leadership, uniting the worlds of literature and business in a symphony of transformation.

Writing a book fosters significant personal and professional growth. The process of researching, writing, and promoting your book requires you to develop new skills and expand your knowledge. This growth can enhance your abilities and open up new opportunities in your career.

The journey of writing isn't just about sharing information; it's about the unquenchable pursuit of knowledge. Authors explore topics deeply, immersing themselves in research, dialogue, and introspection. This exploration fosters a profound understanding of the subject matter and a holistic recognition of its relevance to their personal growth.

The Development of New Skills

The process of writing a book requires a diverse set of skills, including research, writing, editing, communicating and marketing. By undertaking this journey, you can develop and hone these skills, enhancing your overall capabilities. These new skills can be invaluable in your professional life, enabling you to take on new challenges and opportunities.

The culmination of writing a book is not just a finish line; it's a tapestry of effort and dedication woven over time. Completing and publishing a book generates a sense of accomplishment that reverberates through an author's sense of self. This triumph bolsters self-confidence, affirming that the author's dedication and expertise are valued.

As readers engage with the book's content and peers acknowledge the insights shared, authors receive validation of their expertise. The recognition from the audience and industry leaders alike amplifies their self-assuredness in their domain knowledge, further emboldening them to present their ideas with conviction.

The writing journey is albeit riddled with challenges, from grappling with writer's block to navigating critique. Conquering these obstacles fosters resilience, affirming that authors possess the mettle to overcome adversity. These victories against the odds contribute to a profound sense of self-confidence.

Example: Tim Ferriss and "The 4-Hour Workweek"

Tim Ferriss, author of "The 4-Hour Workweek," initially started his journey with limited writing experience. However, the process of writing and promoting his book forced him to develop new skills in research, writing, and marketing. The success of "The 4-Hour Workweek" not only transformed Ferriss's career but also provided him with a platform to explore new ventures, including podcasting, investing, and public speaking. Ferriss's journey illustrates how writing a book can foster significant personal and professional growth.

Expanding Your Knowledge and Expertise

Writing a book requires extensive research and necessitates a deep introspection on your experiences and insights. This process can expand your knowledge and deepen your expertise, providing you with a more comprehensive understanding of your field.

Authors delve into their experiences, dissecting them to unveil valuable insights. This process invites them to reconsider their journey from diverse angles, unraveling layers of meaning that might have remained concealed.

As authors arrange their knowledge in a coherent structure, they often discern connections between seemingly unrelated experiences. This interlinking of ideas not only enriches their insights but illuminates patterns and relationships that might have been overlooked.

Example: Brené Brown and "Daring Greatly"

Brené Brown, a research professor and author, wrote "Daring Greatly: How the Courage to Be Vulnerable Transforms the Way We Live, Love, Parent, and Lead." The process of writing the book required Brown to delve deeply into her research on vulnerability, courage, and shame. This exploration not only expanded her knowledge but also deepened her expertise in these areas. The success of "Daring Greatly" has positioned Brown as a leading authority on vulnerability and leadership, enhancing her professional reputation and opening up new opportunities for research and collaboration.

Creating New Opportunities

The process of writing and promoting a book can create new opportunities for growth and advancement in your career. By establishing yourself as an expert and thought leader, you can attract new opportunities for speaking engagements, consulting, and collaboration.

The allure of a book resonates far and wide, attracting not only readers but fellow experts, professionals, and media attention. The journey of authorship paves the way for a mosaic of networking opportunities, forging connections that span across industries and geographies. The book, akin to a magnetic force, draws like-minded individuals into the author's orbit, expanding their professional ecosystem.

Your book can be a powerful catalyst for professional transformation. It has the potential to tilt the scales in your favor, unlock opportunities for collaboration, and sometimes even pave the way for new career paths such as consulting, teaching, or full-time writing. The impact of a book goes beyond its content, often shaping new and hopeful trajectories.

Example: Daniel Pink and "Drive"

Daniel Pink, an author and speaker, wrote "Drive: The Surprising Truth About What Motivates Us," a book that explores the science of motivation and performance. The success of "Drive" positioned Pink as a leading authority on motivation, leading to numerous speaking engagements, consulting opportunities, and media appearances. Pink's insights have been widely adopted by businesses and educators, enhancing his professional reputation and creating new opportunities for growth and impact.

Building a Personal Brand

Writing a book can also help you build a strong personal brand, enhancing your visibility and reputation. A well-crafted book can showcase your expertise, values, and vision, helping you establish a distinct and compelling personal brand.

A book plays a crucial role in amplifying the author's personal brand. It positions the author as an expert and showcases their unique voice, which is a key part of consistent branding and can set them apart in their field.

Capitalize on the book as a platform to underscore your prowess in a specific niche or industry. Articulate insights, case studies, and expert knowledge that substantiate your authority, cementing your status as a trusted thought leader and fostering a sense of trust among your readers. This trust is a key element in building a strong personal brand.

It's crucial to develop a writing style that resonates with authenticity and distinction. This allows you to infuse your personal perspective into the narrative, offering a fresh and unique angle that sets you apart amidst the sea of voices in your field, inspiring others to find their own unique voice.

Extend the ethos of your personal brand to the book's essence. Align design elements, tone, and content with your brand's aesthetics and values. This congruence reinforces your brand's identity and fosters recognition, making your audience feel reassured and aligned with your brand.

The Significance of a Personal Brand

A strong personal brand can differentiate you from others in your field, making you more recognizable and memorable. It can enhance your credibility and influence, attracting new opportunities and connections. A book can serve as a powerful tool for building and reinforcing your personal brand.

Writing a book provides a powerful platform for introducing innovative ideas, challenging prevailing norms, and shaping the conversation within your field.

This positions you as a thought leader, and you have the opportunity to be at the forefront of your industry by presenting fresh perspectives and proposing forward-thinking strategies. Influential individuals understand the value of writing as a means to share innovative ideas, challenge existing paradigms, and offer unique perspectives. Through compelling arguments, visionary concepts, and forward-thinking solutions, they establish themselves as thought leaders who shape the discourse and agenda in their respective fields.

Publishing a book in your field of expertise immediately sets you apart and elevates your status to an expert. It's tangible proof of your knowledge, experience, and insights. By sharing your expertise in a comprehensive manner, you can establish yourself as an authority in your industry.

By writing a book, you can significantly increase your leadership influence. It serves as a platform to share your vision, insights, and strategies, inspiring and guiding your team while establishing you as a thought leader who can influence the entire industry. This increased visibility brings tremendous respect and recognition, expanding your sphere of leadership influence.

A book allows you to share your personal journey, including the challenges you have overcome and the successes you have achieved. This humanizes you, making you more relatable to your audience. Readers can gain valuable insights from your firsthand experiences, learning from your triumphs and failures.

Writing a book will help amplify your leadership influence, expand your networking opportunities, accelerate career growth, establish a lasting career impact, enhance your personal brand, and contribute to industry knowledge.

It is a powerful endeavor that drives professional growth, recognition, and long-term success.

The role of a book in your strategy to inspire and lead is multifaceted and impactful. It can be a powerful tool to disseminate ideas, share experiences, and provide guidance to a wide audience, making it an integral part of your leadership approach, enhancing your personal brand even further.

Example: Simon Sinek and "Start with Why"

Simon Sinek, a leadership expert, authored "Start with Why: How Great Leaders Inspire Everyone to Take Action," a book that explores the importance of understanding the purpose behind your work. Sinek's book has become a bestseller and has established him as a leading authority on leadership and motivation.

Through his book, Sinek has built a strong personal brand, attracting speaking engagements, consulting opportunities, and media appearances. His insights have resonated with leaders and organizations around the world, enhancing his reputation and influence.

Inspiring and Empowering Others

Writing a book allows you to inspire and empower others by sharing your knowledge and experiences. Your insights can provide valuable guidance and encouragement to those who are on similar paths, helping them overcome challenges and achieve their goals.

The Impact of Inspiration

Inspiring others can be incredibly fulfilling, as it allows you to make a positive impact on their lives. Your book can serve as a source of motivation and encouragement, helping readers believe in their potential and pursue their dreams.

Example: Elizabeth Gilbert and "Eat, Pray, Love"

Elizabeth Gilbert, an author, penned "Eat, Pray, Love: One Woman's Search for Everything Across Italy, India, and Indonesia," a memoir that chronicles her journey of self-discovery following a difficult divorce. The book resonated with millions of readers around the world, inspiring them to seek out their own paths to happiness and fulfillment. Gilbert's candid storytelling and willingness to share her vulnerabilities provided readers with a sense of connection and hope. "Eat, Pray, Love" has inspired countless individuals to pursue their dreams and embark on their own journeys of self-discovery, highlighting the profound impact a book can have in inspiring and empowering others.

Creating a Sense of Fulfillment

Ultimately, writing a book can create a deep sense of fulfillment, as it allows you to achieve a significant personal and professional milestone. The process of sharing your knowledge and experiences, making a positive impact on others, and leaving a lasting legacy can bring immense satisfaction and joy.

The Joy of Accomplishment

The sense of accomplishment that comes from completing a book is unparalleled. It's a testament to your hard work, dedication, and perseverance. This achievement can boost your self-esteem and confidence, reinforcing your belief in your abilities and potential.

Example: Michelle Obama and "Becoming"

Michelle Obama, former First Lady of the United States, authored "Becoming," a memoir that chronicles her life journey, from her childhood in Chicago to her years in the White House. The process of writing "Becoming" allowed Obama to reflect on her experiences and share her story with the world.

The book has become a global bestseller, inspiring millions of readers and making a significant impact. For Obama, the sense of fulfillment that comes from sharing her journey and making a positive impact on others is evident in her words and actions.

Numerous studies and expert opinions support the benefits of writing a book for personal and professional fulfillment. According to a study published in the Journal of Positive Psychology, achieving significant personal milestones, such as writing a book, is associated with increased well-being and life satisfaction. The study found that individuals who achieve these milestones report higher levels of happiness, self-esteem, and overall life satisfaction. Furthermore, a report by the American Psychological Association (APA) highlights the importance of personal growth and achievement in fostering a sense of fulfillment and well-being. The report states that engaging in meaningful and challenging activities, such as writing a book, can enhance personal and professional development, leading to greater fulfillment and life satisfaction.

Writing a book can bring immense personal and professional fulfillment. It serves as a significant milestone, a platform for sharing your journey and insights, and a means of leaving a lasting legacy. By undertaking the journey of writing a book, you can achieve personal growth, create new opportunities, and inspire others, ultimately making a meaningful impact on your field and beyond.

"The only limits you have are the ones you put on yourself. So, never let fear stop you from reaching your potential."

Key Takeaways

- **Achieving Personal Milestones**: Writing a book is a significant personal milestone that can bring immense satisfaction and boost your self-esteem and confidence.

- **Sharing Your Journey and Experiences**: Writing a book allows you to share your journey and experiences with a broader audience, providing valuable insights and inspiration.

- **Leaving a Legacy**: A book can serve as a lasting legacy, preserving your knowledge and experiences for future generations and leaving a lasting impact in your field.

- **Personal and Professional Growth**: The process of writing a book can foster significant personal and professional growth, enhancing your skills and expanding your knowledge.

- **Creating New Opportunities**: Writing and promoting a book can create new opportunities for growth and advancement in your career.

- **Building a Personal Brand**: A well-crafted book can help you build a strong personal brand, enhancing your visibility and reputation.

- **Inspiring and Empowering Others**: Writing a book allows you to inspire and empower others by sharing your knowledge and experiences.

- **Creating a Sense of Fulfillment**: The process of writing a book and making a positive impact on others can create a deep sense of fulfillment and joy.

Working harder doesn't guarantee success—**positioning, visibility, and influence** do. Just like in business, writing a book helps you **stand out, build authority, and create new opportunities** without the constant grind. If you're ready to shift from just working hard to making a lasting impact, **scan the QR code** and take the next step toward growth!

7

HANDLING CRITICISM, FEEDBACK, AND PUBLIC REACTION

"If you don't want criticism, do nothing, say nothing, and be nothing."
—**Elbert Hubbard**

For entrepreneurs-turned-authors, publishing a book can be a thrilling milestone—until the first wave of public opinion crashes in. Suddenly, there are reviews, comments on social media, interview questions, and letters to your inbox. Some of it's glowing, some neutral, and some downright harsh. While this feedback loop can be intimidating, it also holds untapped opportunities for growth and deeper audience engagement. The key is learning to handle critique—both constructive and negative—in a way that strengthens your reputation, clarifies your message, and reinforces your relationship with readers.

This chapter explores how to navigate these varied reactions effectively. You'll learn practical strategies for transforming criticism into lessons, amplifying positive endorsements, and maintaining your composure in the face of public scrutiny.

By addressing criticism in a thoughtful, transparent manner, you can not only preserve the credibility you've built with your book but also strengthen it.

Understanding the Nature of Public Feedback: The Good, the Bad, and the Indifferent

Positive Feedback: When the praise comes in—online reviews, social media shout-outs, private messages—it can be a tremendous morale booster. More importantly, it's your chance to see what aspects of your book resonate most. Did readers love the personal anecdotes? The unique frameworks you shared? Those are signals for future products or expansions of your brand.

Negative Feedback: Not all negative reactions are created equal. Some critiques are thoughtful and detailed, pointing out legitimate areas for improvement, while others might be malicious or based on misunderstandings. Distinguishing one from the other is crucial.

Indifference or Silence: Sometimes, the most challenging form of feedback is a lack of response. If readers aren't commenting, reviewing, or discussing, you're not receiving the engagement that can catalyze word-of-mouth marketing. Interpreting the reasons behind silence helps you adjust your strategy, be it in marketing or in clarifying your content.

A Reality Check on Reader Engagement

If your book has received only a handful of reviews, don't be discouraged—it's not a reflection of its impact. In fact, only **about 1% of readers leave a written review,** while approximately **10% may leave a star rating**. The vast majority remain silent, even if they found value in your work. Understanding this helps put feedback into perspective: a few negative or indifferent reviews don't define your book's success. Instead, focus on engaging with your audience and encouraging thoughtful responses to build a more representative picture of your readership.

Public vs. Private Reactions

Public Domain

Reviews on Amazon, Goodreads, social media mentions—these are visible for all to see. Potential readers will often look at these impressions before deciding whether to invest in your book. Responding (or not responding) to public feedback shapes your image as an author and entrepreneur.

Private Feedback

Emails, direct messages, and one-on-one conversations can offer more intimate critiques or praise. Because this feedback is less filtered for an audience, it's often more honest and detailed. Addressing these private channels with care can convert casual readers into brand ambassadors or satisfied clients.

Why Criticism and Feedback Matter

Evolution of Your Thought Leadership

When someone points out inconsistencies or challenges your premises, it forces you to revisit your conclusions. You may find fresh angles for future writing or correct oversights in your current edition. Seen through the right lens, negative feedback can be the impetus for growth and deeper industry expertise.

Embracing a Learning Mindset

- Ask clarifying questions: "Could you expand on what didn't work for you?"
- Acknowledge valid points and pledge to adapt.
- Resist the urge to defend every line; let the conversation breathe.

Strengthening Credibility and Authenticity

A well-handled critique can enhance rather than diminish your credibility. Publicly owning up to an oversight—say, a misquoted statistic—demonstrates integrity. Likewise, engaging respectfully with harsh comments can display empathy and patience, traits that readers respect and remember.

Building a Loyal Community

Readers who see you listening and responding are more likely to remain loyal to your work. They appreciate being acknowledged, and fellow audience members observe your brand values in action. Over time, constructive dialogue fosters a community that genuinely supports your message.

Types of Criticism You May Encounter

1. Constructive, Specific Critiques

Example: A reader points out a contradiction in your marketing framework, offering evidence from a different case study.

Response Strategy
1. Thank them for their insight.
2. Ask clarifying questions to show genuine interest.
3. Consider how to address the gap—maybe in a blog post or in a revised edition.

2. Vague or Emotional Criticism

Example: "Your book just isn't any good. I couldn't get into it." No specifics given.

Response Strategy
1. Politely request details: "I'd love to know more about what didn't resonate."
2. If no further clarity comes, you can end the exchange gracefully without dwelling.

3. Personal Attacks or Trolls

Examples: "You're a fraud who shouldn't be writing about entrepreneurship." OR A user spreading rumors unrelated to your content.

Response Strategy
1. Resist impulsive emotional replies.
2. If it's a genuine platform-based violation, you may report it.
3. In some cases, ignoring or offering a calm, brief response might be best.

4. Passive-Aggressive "Praise"

Example: "Well, I guess if you're new to business, this book might be okay, but real entrepreneurs won't learn much."

Response Strategy
1. Thank them for reading.
2. Highlight any valid points.
3. Avoid letting the tone derail your brand composure.

Strategies for Responding
1. Pause Before You Reply
When you first read criticism—particularly if it's harsh or personal—your emotions might flare. Take a beat (or a day) to let your initial reactions simmer down. Rash, defensive responses can escalate tensions and harm your brand.

2. Start with Empathy and Gratitude
A simple "Thank you for taking the time to share your thoughts" can disarm an upset reader. Recognizing the effort they made to provide feedback (even if critical) sets a positive tone. If the criticism is valid, express genuine appreciation for their perspective.

3. Clarify Misunderstandings

If the comment indicates a misunderstanding of your book's content, kindly clarify. Sometimes a negative review stems from confusion over what your book promised vs. what it delivered. Correct the misconception politely. If you realize your marketing materials or introduction might have been ambiguous, make a note to fix those issues.

4. Offer Solutions or Next Steps

Where possible, lead the critic or the audience to a solution. If they complained about missing examples, point them to an additional resource on your website. If they wanted deeper content on a sub-topic, let them know a future blog post or podcast episode is in the works.

> "The biggest problem with communication is the illusion that it has taken place. When receiving criticism, don't just hear—listen. It's an opportunity to understand, not just to respond."
> - **Deborah Tannen (Author, Linguist, Communication Expert)**

5. Know When to Step Away

• **Trolling:** If someone is there only to provoke, any engagement can fuel more attacks.

• **Redundant Cycles**: After you've answered concerns comprehensively, continuing the debate can be counterproductive.

• **Professional Boundaries**: It's okay to enforce them. Your brand identity should stand on respect, both given and received.

"Balance is key to success. So, find ways to blend your professional and personal life and maintain a healthy work-life balance."

Leveraging Positive Feedback

1. Amplifying the Praise
- **Testimonials & Endorsements**

When a glowing review appears, ask for permission to feature it on your website, social media, or in a future edition of your book. Potential readers often look for credible endorsements before purchasing.

- **Video or Audio Testimonials**

If feasible, invite satisfied readers to record a short clip about the impact your book had on their business or mindset. These genuine endorsements are powerful trust signals.

2. Encouraging Word-of-Mouth

A personal recommendation is invaluable. Encourage engaged readers to share their experiences with friends, or invite them to discuss your book on their own channels. Provide shareable quotes or highlight reels to make it easy for them.

Incorporating Feedback into Your Content and Business

1. Second Editions or "Updates"

Sometimes, negative or constructive criticism flags an area that needs deeper coverage, more case studies, or updated data. If enough readers echo the same concern, you might revise your manuscript for the next printing or produce a supplementary online resource.

2. Pivoting or Strengthening Your Entrepreneurial Offerings

Critique about your methodology might uncover an unaddressed pain point in your audience. That's an opportunity to expand your brand—maybe through coaching sessions, digital courses, or an entire new spinoff product that focuses on that gap.

3. Blog Posts, Podcasts, and Follow-Up Engagement

Detailing how you addressed a given critique can itself be compelling content. A blog post titled "Top 5 Reader Concerns About My Book—and What I've Learned" not only shows humility but also fosters deeper trust.

Handling Public Crises or Controversies

1. Anticipating the Crisis

If your book tackles a hot-button topic or challenges a widely held industry belief, you should anticipate a certain amount of pushback or controversy. Have a measured plan for responding publicly—possibly a dedicated FAQ or statement if your stance is likely to spark debate.

2. Transparency and Honesty

In a fast-moving social media uproar, denial or stonewalling can worsen matters. Instead, quickly clarify your perspective, correct misinformation, and demonstrate willingness to hear opposing views. This doesn't require diluting your core beliefs; it's about open communication.

3. Lean on Your Support Network

If you've built relationships with readers, influencers, and peers, they can help defend or contextualize your message. Encouraging them to share their positive experiences or interpretations can mitigate the impact of a wave of negative attention.

The Emotional Side of Criticism

1. Managing Personal Feelings

Criticism can sting, especially if you've poured your heart into the book. Remind yourself that feedback—even if voiced harshly—often reflects the user's point of view and not your inherent value. Seek a trusted friend, mentor, or a therapist if you find negative comments shaking your self-confidence.

2. Avoiding Over-Identification with the Book

Yes, the content is personal, but your identity extends beyond what's on the page. Mentally separating your self-worth from your published material can help you maintain perspective and resilience.

3. Celebrating Progress

Balance the inevitable negative voices with reminders of how far you've come—finishing a manuscript, launching your book, and hearing from the readers you've helped. Keep a folder of positive messages or reviews for those days when negativity weighs heavily.

Long-Term Reputation Management

1. Consistency in Voice and Tone

Whether responding on social media or in an Amazon comment thread, maintain a consistent, respectful tone. Over time, readers will associate your name with a specific style of interaction—hopefully one rooted in professionalism, empathy, and clarity.

2. Updating Your Public Platforms

If you adapt or revise your stance based on repeated criticisms, share those changes publicly. Post an announcement on social media, update your website, or add a note in your book's next edition. This demonstrates accountability and evolution.

3. Monitoring Tools

Consider using social media monitoring or reputation management tools. They can alert you to spikes in mentions or trends in sentiment. You'll spot potential crises early, see recurring suggestions, and jump into constructive discussions before they pass you by.

A Resource Guide: Reputation Tracking and Feedback Management Tools

Whether you're an entrepreneur, author, business leader, or public figure, managing your online reputation is a critical task. To make this process easier for you, I've put together this list of tools and platforms that can help you track feedback, monitor brand mentions, manage reviews, and handle public perception across digital and media channels.

1. Social Listening & Brand Monitoring

These tools help track brand mentions, monitor conversations, and assess sentiment across social media, blogs, forums, and news sites.

> **Free Tools:**
> - **Google Alerts** (alerts.google.com): Tracks brand, book, or name mentions online.
> - **Social Mention** (socialmention.com): Free tool for real-time brand monitoring and sentiment analysis.

Premium Tools:

• **Brand24** (brand24.com): AI-powered social listening and sentiment analysis.

• **Mention** (mention.com): Monitors brand mentions across social platforms, blogs, and news sites.

• **Awario** (awario.com): In-depth sentiment analysis and competitor tracking.

• **Talkwalker** (talkwalker.com): Advanced analytics for media monitoring and crisis management.

• **Meltwater** (meltwater.com): Tracks media coverage and online reputation.

2. Review & Feedback Management

For authors, entrepreneurs, and businesses, online reviews shape public perception. These tools help collect, monitor, and respond to customer feedback.

• **Trustpilot** (trustpilot.com): Manages and responds to online reviews.

• **Reputology** (reputology.com): Aggregates and analyzes customer reviews.

• **Yotpo** (yotpo.com): Helps businesses collect and display reviews.

• **Podium** (podium.com): Centralized review and messaging management.

• **Review Trackers** (reviewtrackers.com): Consolidates reviews from various platforms into one dashboard.

3. Media & PR Monitoring

These platforms track **news articles, media coverage, and press mentions**, helping individuals and brands stay ahead of public perception.

• **Cision** (cision.com): PR software for tracking press mentions and influencer engagement.

• **Critical Mention** (criticalmention.com): Monitors TV, radio, and online news sources.

- **Muck Rack** (muckrack.com): Tracks media coverage and journalist activity.
- **Help a Reporter Out** (HARO) (helpareporter.com): Connects experts with journalists for media exposure

4. Reputation Management & Crisis Response

These services help suppress negative content, improve online image, and manage public perception.

- **BrandYourself** (brandyourself.com): Cleans up negative search results and personal branding.
- **NetReputation** (netreputation.com): Specializes in online reputation repair.
- **ReputationDefender** (reputationdefender.com): Monitors search results and brand credibility.
- **SentiOne** (sentione.com): AI-driven crisis management for brands and public figures.
- **NiceJob** (nicejob.com): Automates reputation management and customer feedback collection.

5. Comprehensive Reputation & Sentiment Analysis

These platforms offer in-depth insights into public sentiment, online visibility, and brand perception.

- **Sprout Social** (sproutsocial.com): Social media management with brand reputation tracking.
- **Hootsuite Insights** (hootsuite.com): Monitors online sentiment powered by Brandwatch.
- **SEMrush Brand Monitoring** (semrush.com): Tracks brand mentions and online reputation.
- **BuzzSumo** (buzzsumo.com): Analyzes content performance and brand reach.

This resource guide provides an actionable approach to reputation tracking and management. Whether you're an entrepreneur, or business leader, leveraging these tools will help you stay informed, protect your brand, and manage public perception effectively.

Putting It All into Practice: An Action Framework

1. Categorize Feedback: Sort each comment, review, or mention into categories: Positive, Constructive, Unclear, or Irrelevant/Trolling. This helps you see patterns in how your book is received.

2. Respond Strategically: Address essential points where you can clarify misunderstandings or provide extra value. Don't get lost in endless back-and-forth with trolls.

3. Document and Reflect: Keep a record of the most frequent critiques or compliments. Look for repeated themes that might warrant a future blog post, second edition, or new service.

4. Plan Revisions and Expansion: Use the feedback to improve your manuscript, your brand messaging, and your business offerings.

5. Celebrate the Wins: Curate positive feedback. Share testimonials publicly (with permission) and use them to attract new readers or clients.

Criticism, feedback, and public reaction aren't barriers to your entrepreneurial journey—they're a natural consequence of putting your ideas and convictions into the public sphere. By staying open to dialogue, addressing misunderstandings constructively, and calmly meeting aggression when it arises, you can mold even challenging situations into catalysts for growth.

Your readers, followers, and partners will pay close attention to how you handle these pivotal moments. Show them that your brand isn't just about a single viewpoint cast in stone; it's about learning, adapting, and continuing to serve—no matter what hurdles appear. In the process, you'll likely discover new depths of credibility, authenticity, and loyalty in the community that grows around your work.

"When handled with courage and grace, criticism and feedback become steppingstones to deeper connection, refined expertise, and a reputation for integrity—everything an entrepreneur-author needs to succeed in a world that values both bold ideas and thoughtful engagement."
— **Raam Anand**

"Feedback is the breakfast of champions."
-**Ken Blanchard, Leadership and Communication expert**

[YouTube Link](#)

8

STRATEGIC BUSINESS GROWTH

"In the business world, the rearview mirror is always clearer than the windshield."
—**Warren Buffett**

In the dynamic and often unpredictable world of startups, finding strategic ways to fuel business growth is paramount. Imagine you're at a pivotal meeting with potential investors, and instead of relying solely on a pitch deck, you present them with a copy of your book that outlines your vision, strategy, and the innovative solutions your company offers. This book not only serves as a comprehensive resource but also as a testament to your thought leadership and expertise. Writing a book can be a game-changing strategy for driving business growth by generating leads, attracting new revenue streams, and establishing your brand as a leader in the industry, providing a sense of security and confidence in your business's future. Beyond that, it opens doors to speaking engagements, partnerships, and media opportunities, further expanding your influence and network.

Lead Generation

A book can be a powerful tool for lead generation. It can attract potential clients, partners, and investors interested in your insights and expertise. By sharing valuable content that addresses the needs and challenges of your target audience, you can generate interest and build a pipeline of qualified leads.

The book can be distributed at expos, workshops, and events and even be used as a prize during networking opportunities. This will help inform strangers of your expertise and attract prospective clients or customers interested in your book. When the right person receives your book containing all relevant information and a call to action, they can build knowledge, trust, and rapport by reading and connecting with you, ultimately leading them to contact you for further collaboration.

Lead generation can be achieved by showcasing excerpts from your book through various marketing strategies and online engagements. This involves sharing the content of your book to provide valuable insights and strategies from your expert point of view, offering practical advice or relatable anecdotes, and establishing a rapport that helps you connect with your audience. Ultimately, this can result in better sales and revenue, giving you a reason to be optimistic and hopeful for the future of your startup.

Using Your Book to Attract New Clients, Partners, and Investors

Your book can serve as an extended business card, providing potential clients, partners, and investors with a comprehensive overview of your expertise and vision. It can help you establish credibility and build trust, making it easier to convert leads into meaningful business relationships.

As reiterated multiple times so far, a book is a powerful tool that establishes your authority and cements your position in your industry. The key role of your Book as a Strategy (BaaS) is to showcase your expertise, insights, and solution-oriented perspective, which in turn attracts new clients to your products or services. Partners are drawn to your offerings, vision, mission, and depth of expertise, all of which are clearly demonstrated in your book. Investors can gain a clear projection of the potential you hold as an author, further enhancing your credibility and opening up numerous collaborative opportunities. Your authored and published book is a crucial asset in showcasing your expertise, building relationships and networks, and attracting new collaborative opportunities. Use it to its full potential to grow your business, just like Tony Robbins.

Example: Tony Robbins and "Money: Master the Game"

Robbins, a renowned life coach and entrepreneur, authored "Money: Master the Game: 7 Simple Steps to Financial Freedom," a book that offers practical financial advice and strategies for achieving financial independence. The book's success helped Robbins attract a new audience of clients and investors interested in his financial services. By providing valuable insights and actionable advice, Robbins was able to generate leads and build relationships with individuals and organizations seeking financial guidance. The book's success also led to numerous speaking engagements and media appearances, further expanding Robbins' reach and influence.

Incorporating Your Book into Marketing Campaigns

Integrating your book into your marketing campaigns can amplify your message and reach a broader audience. By leveraging the content of your book in various marketing channels, such as social media, email newsletters, and webinars, you can create a cohesive and compelling narrative that attracts and engages potential clients and partners.

Your book is an incredibly valuable marketing asset. You can get as creative and experimental as possible. There are no limits! You can extract key points and concepts from your book's chapters to create blog posts, articles, video series, or even podcasts. Offer free consultation or sample chapters to your subscribers or interest groups. Showcase your social media presence with excerpts from your books, sharing bite-sized information in the form of quotes, images, or key takeaways from your book. For example, you can create visually appealing quote cards or share pictures of your book cover with a brief description. Utilize Instagram stories, reels, YouTube shorts, partner with influencers or industry experts, and make your social media promotion interactive to engage your audience. Use your book's prominence and relevance to enhance your website, host workshops and conferences, and organize events. Your book could be an extremely crucial marketing asset – so be bold and try new things!

Example: Neil Patel and "Hustle"

Neil Patel, a digital marketing expert and co-author of "Hustle: The Power to Charge Your Life with Money, Meaning, and Momentum," effectively incorporated his book into his marketing campaigns. Patel used excerpts from the book in his blog posts, social media updates, and email newsletters to attract and engage his audience. He also hosted webinars and live events based on the book's content, providing additional value to his followers. This integrated approach helped Patel generate leads and build a strong community around his brand, ultimately driving business growth.

Additional Revenue streams from Book Sales, Speaking Engagements, and Consulting

Publishing a book can open up new revenue streams beyond your core business. Book sales, speaking engagements, consulting, and workshops are just a few of the ways you can monetize your expertise and create additional income streams.

A successful book can generate significant revenue from book sales, especially if it becomes a bestseller. Additionally, authors are often invited to speak at conferences, seminars, and corporate events, providing another lucrative revenue stream. Consulting opportunities can also arise from your book, as organizations seek your expertise to implement the strategies and insights you've shared.

Beyond the immediate sales, the legacy of a book morphs into an enduring wellspring of revenue. Its content can be repurposed into courses, workshops, or consultation services, ushering in diverse income streams. The book evolves into a cornerstone of the author's entrepreneurial pursuits.

Example: Guy Kawasaki and "The Art of the Start"

Guy Kawasaki, a venture capitalist and entrepreneur, authored "The Art of the Start: The Time-Tested, Battle-Hardened Guide for Anyone Starting Anything," a book that offers practical advice for entrepreneurs. The book's success led to numerous speaking engagements and consulting opportunities for Kawasaki. Organizations and startups sought his expertise to help them navigate the challenges of launching and growing a business. The revenue generated from book sales, speaking engagements, and consulting contributed significantly to Kawasaki's overall business growth.

Opportunities for Workshops and Seminars

Your book can serve as the foundation for workshops and seminars, providing a structured framework for delivering valuable content to your audience. These events can be a significant source of revenue and help you build deeper relationships with clients and partners.

Example: Michael E. Gerber and "The E-Myth Revisited"

Michael E. Gerber, author of "The E-Myth Revisited: Why Most Small Businesses Don't Work and What to Do About It," used his book as the basis for workshops and seminars aimed at small business owners. Gerber's workshops provided practical guidance on building successful businesses, drawing on the principles outlined in his book. These events became a significant revenue stream for Gerber and helped him build a loyal following of small business owners who benefited from his insights and expertise.

Enhancing Brand Visibility

A book can significantly enhance your brand's visibility by positioning you as a thought leader in your industry. Media coverage, guest articles, and speaking engagements can amplify your message and reach a broader audience, increasing your brand's recognition and credibility.

A book serves as a testament to your knowledge and commitment to your field. It establishes trust and credibility with potential partners or media outlets, who may view the publication as a sign of stability and thought leadership. This credibility can be a decisive factor in forming your image as an industry expert and making ways for partnerships, as businesses often seek reliable and knowledgeable allies. This further solidifies your stand in your industry, making you the go-to expert for interviews and articles, as well as seminars and conferences.

Gaining Media Attention and Coverage

Publishing a book can attract significant media attention, providing you with opportunities to share your story and insights with a broader audience. Media coverage can amplify your message and enhance your brand's visibility, attracting potential clients, partners, and investors.

Example: Tim Ferriss and "The 4-Hour Workweek"

Tim Ferriss, author of "The 4-Hour Workweek: Escape 9-5, Live Anywhere, and Join the New Rich," gained extensive media coverage following the book's release. Ferriss appeared on major news networks, talk shows, and in prominent publications, sharing his insights on productivity and lifestyle design. This media attention significantly enhanced Ferriss's visibility and helped him build a strong personal brand. The success of "The 4-Hour Workweek" also led to numerous speaking engagements and consulting opportunities, further expanding Ferriss's reach and influence.

Becoming a Go-To Expert for Interviews and Articles

Publishing a book positions you as an expert in your field, making you a go-to source for interviews and articles. Journalists and media outlets often seek out authors for their insights and expertise, providing you with additional opportunities to promote your startup and its mission.

Example: Gary Vaynerchuk and "Crush It!"

Gary Vaynerchuk, a serial entrepreneur and social media expert, authored "Crush It! Why NOW Is the Time to Cash In on Your Passion." The book's success positioned Vaynerchuk as a leading authority on digital marketing and personal branding. As a result, he has become a sought-after speaker and media personality, regularly appearing on major news outlets and industry podcasts. These opportunities have allowed Vaynerchuk to promote his businesses, VaynerMedia and VaynerX, enhancing their reputation and attracting new clients.

Building Long-Term Relationships

A book can help you build long-term relationships with clients, partners, and investors by providing them with valuable insights and demonstrating your expertise. These relationships can lead to repeat business, referrals, and ongoing collaborations, driving sustainable business growth.

A book can serve as a long-term asset for your brand, continually generating interest and opportunities long after its initial release. It can be a key element in your long-term brand strategy, providing a foundation for future content and marketing efforts. Regularly revisiting and updating the book's content can keep it relevant and continue to attract new audiences, ensuring sustained visibility and influence.

Demonstrating Your Commitment to Value Creation

By sharing your knowledge and expertise through a book, you demonstrate your commitment to creating value for your clients, partners, and investors. This commitment can build trust and loyalty, fostering long-term relationships that contribute to your business's growth.

Example: Jay Baer and "Youtility"

Jay Baer, a marketing consultant and author, wrote "Youtility: Why Smart Marketing Is About Help Not Hype," a book that emphasizes the importance of providing value to customers. Baer's book has resonated with businesses seeking to improve their marketing strategies by focusing on customer needs. By sharing his insights and practical advice, Baer has built long-term relationships with clients who trust his expertise and value his commitment to helping them succeed. These relationships have led to repeat business, referrals, and ongoing collaborations, driving sustainable growth for Baer's consulting firm.

Creating a Community Around Your Brand

A book can help you create a community around your brand, bringing together like-minded individuals who share your vision and values. Readers who connect with your message may become loyal followers and advocates, participating in discussions, attending events, and promoting your content. Engaging with this community through book signings, Q&A sessions, and social media interactions can foster a sense of loyalty, further enhancing your brand's visibility and impact. This community can become a powerful advocate for your brand, promoting your business through word-of-mouth and creating a sense of belonging.

Example: Seth Godin and "Tribes"

Seth Godin, a marketing guru, authored "Tribes: We Need You to Lead Us," a book that explores the power of community and leadership. Godin's book has inspired countless individuals to create and lead their own tribes, bringing together people who share common interests and goals. By building a community around his brand, Godin has created a loyal following that actively promotes his books, courses, and events. This community has become a powerful advocate for Godin's brand, driving business growth and enhancing his influence.

Leveraging Your Book for Strategic Partnerships

Your book can serve as a valuable tool for establishing strategic partnerships with other businesses and organizations. By showcasing your expertise and vision, you can attract partners who align with your values and goals, creating opportunities for collaboration and mutual growth. Strategic partnerships can amplify your brand's reach, enhance its credibility, and drive innovation by pooling resources and expertise from different entities.

Attracting Partners Who Share Your Vision

A well-written book can attract partners who share your vision and values, creating opportunities for strategic collaborations that drive business growth. By highlighting your expertise and innovative approaches, you can demonstrate the value of partnering with your startup.

Potential partners are more likely to engage with you when they see the depth of knowledge and the unique perspective you bring to the table. This alignment can lead to collaborations that not only enhance your brand but also foster innovation and drive industry change.

Example: Reid Hoffman and "Blitzscaling"

Reid Hoffman, co-founder of LinkedIn, authored "Blitzscaling: The Lightning-Fast Path to Building Massively Valuable Companies," a book that explores the strategy of scaling companies rapidly. Hoffman's book has attracted numerous partners interested in implementing blitzscaling strategies in their own businesses. By showcasing his expertise and vision, Hoffman has established strategic partnerships with organizations that align with his goals, creating opportunities for mutual growth and innovation.

Collaborating on Joint Ventures and Initiatives

Your book can also open up opportunities for joint ventures and initiatives with other businesses and organizations. By leveraging your expertise and insights, you can create collaborative projects that drive business growth and innovation.

Example: Eric Ries and "The Startup Way"

Eric Ries, author of "The Lean Startup," followed up with "The Startup Way: How Modern Companies Use Entrepreneurial Management to Transform Culture and Drive Long-Term Growth." Ries's books have led to numerous joint ventures and initiatives with established companies seeking to implement lean startup methodologies. By collaborating with these organizations, Ries has been able to drive business growth and innovation, creating new opportunities for his consulting firm and enhancing his influence in the industry.

Enhancing Customer Loyalty

A book can help you enhance customer loyalty by providing valuable insights and demonstrating your commitment to their success. Customers who feel valued and supported are more likely to remain loyal to your brand and recommend your business to others.

Providing Value-Added Content

By offering valuable content that addresses your customers' needs and challenges, your book can reinforce their loyalty and trust in your brand. This value-added content can help customers achieve their goals and solve their problems, creating a positive experience that fosters loyalty.

Example: Marcus Sheridan and "They Ask, You Answer"

Marcus Sheridan, a marketing expert, authored "They Ask, You Answer: A Revolutionary Approach to Inbound Sales, Content Marketing, and Today's Digital Consumer," a book that provides practical advice on addressing customer questions and needs through content marketing. Sheridan's book has helped countless businesses improve their marketing strategies and achieve better results. By providing valuable insights and actionable advice, Sheridan has built strong relationships with his clients, enhancing their loyalty and trust in his expertise.

Building a Community of Loyal Customers

A book can help you build a community of loyal customers who actively engage with your brand and promote your business through word-of-mouth. This community can become a powerful advocate for your brand, driving growth and creating a sense of belonging.

Example: Chris Guillebeau and "The Art of Non-Conformity"

Chris Guillebeau, an author and entrepreneur, wrote "The Art of Non-Conformity: Set Your Own Rules, Live the Life You Want, and Change the World," a book that encourages readers to embrace unconventional paths and pursue their dreams. Guillebeau's book has inspired a global community of individuals who share his vision of non-conformity and adventure. This community actively engages with Guillebeau's brand, promoting his books, courses, and events through word-of-mouth. The sense of belonging and shared values has created a loyal customer base that drives business growth and enhances Guillebeau's influence.

Numerous studies and expert opinions support the benefits of writing a book for driving strategic business growth. According to a study published in the Journal of Business Research, thought leadership, demonstrated through authored content such as books, significantly enhances credibility and trust. This increased credibility can lead to greater visibility and reputation, attracting new customers, investors, and partners.

Furthermore, a report by the Content Marketing Institute highlights the importance of thought leadership in driving business growth. The report states that thought leadership, demonstrated through authored content such as books, significantly enhances credibility and trust, leading to stronger and more productive relationships with stakeholders.

Writing a book can significantly drive strategic business growth. It serves as a powerful tool for lead generation, revenue generation, brand visibility, relationship building, community creation, strategic partnerships, and customer loyalty. By sharing your knowledge and experiences, you can create meaningful connections, drive your business forward, and make a lasting impact in your industry.

> *"If you don't drive your business, you will be driven out of business."*
> — **B.C. Forbes (Founder, Forbes Magazine)**

> *"The secret of change is to focus all your energy not on fighting the old, but on building the new."*
> — **Socrates**

Key Takeaways

- **Lead Generation:** A book can be a powerful tool for lead generation, attracting potential clients, partners, and investors who are interested in your insights and expertise.

- **Revenue Streams:** Publishing a book can open up new revenue streams beyond your core business, including book sales, speaking engagements, consulting, and workshops.

- **Enhancing Brand Visibility:** A book can significantly enhance your brand's visibility by positioning you as a thought leader in your industry.

- **Building Long-Term Relationships:** A book can help you build long-term relationships with clients, partners, and investors by providing them with valuable insights and demonstrating your expertise.

- **Creating a Community Around Your Brand:** A book can help you create a community around your brand, bringing together like-minded individuals who share your vision and values.

- **Leveraging Your Book for Strategic Partnerships:** Your book can serve as a valuable tool for establishing strategic partnerships with other businesses and organizations.

- **Enhancing Customer Loyalty:** A book can help you enhance customer loyalty by providing valuable insights and demonstrating your commitment to their success.

[YouTube Link](https://www.youtube.com)

9
MONETIZING YOUR BOOK BEYOND ROYALTIES

"You don't have to be the biggest name to earn the biggest impact—or the biggest profits—from your book. You just have to be the one who sees the full potential..."

—**Raam Anand**

For many entrepreneurs, the idea of writing a book seems like the ultimate brand-building move. You spend months (or even years) pouring your experiences, insights, and convictions into a manuscript, and when it finally hits the shelves (physical or virtual), your initial revenue is likely to come from one source: book sales. These royalties can be a welcome influx of cash—especially if your book gains momentum—but focusing solely on sales is somewhat shortsighted.

In reality, the power of a well-written, strategically positioned book extends far beyond copies sold. The text you've authored can become a gateway to diverse streams of income, from speaking and consulting to digital products, corporate partnerships, and more.

This chapter uncovers the multiple pathways to monetize your book beyond the traditional royalty model. You'll discover how to leverage your content into workshops, training, coaching, online courses, and licensing deals, among others. The goal is to help you realize that authorship isn't just about a product—it's about creating an entire ecosystem centered on your unique expertise. By the end of this chapter, you'll have a clear roadmap for transforming your manuscript into a multifaceted revenue generator, all while remaining faithful to the mission, integrity, and personal voice that make your book truly yours.

Let's explore **ten big ideas** to understand this concept:
- The Bigger Picture: Why Go Beyond Royalties?
- Consulting and Coaching: Translating Ideas Into Action
- Paid Speaking: Beyond the Podium
- Creating Digital Products: Courses, Webinars, Memberships
- Corporate Partnerships, Sponsorships, and Licensing
- Building a Personalized Ecosystem: Masterminds, Live Events, and Retreats
- Revenue Funnel: Key Insights
- Sustainable Monetization: Mindset Shift
- Avoiding Pitfalls: 4 Big Mistakes
- Action Steps: Your Monetization Roadmap

Big Idea #1: The Bigger Picture: Why Go Beyond Royalties?

1. Expanding Brand Influence

A book establishes you as a thought leader or subject-matter expert in your entrepreneurial niche. However, the scale of that influence depends on the platforms and activities you choose after publication. Monetizing beyond royalties is not merely a chase for profit; it's an opportunity to expand your brand's reach and reputation. For instance, imagine turning your book's central thesis into an on-demand online course or being invited to speak at industry conferences because you've developed a recognized framework. Each new endeavor circles back, driving fresh audiences to your book—and vice versa.

2. Diversifying Revenue Streams

Every experienced entrepreneur knows the adage: *Never depend on a single source of revenue.* Books are cyclical products—your sales may spike during a launch or after a media mention but gradually slow over time. By establishing additional income channels—like corporate training or mastermind groups—you cushion yourself against the unpredictability of book sales. This diversification fosters stability, supporting you through market ups and downs.

3. Deepening Audience Engagement

While a reader gleaning insights from a page is impactful, the relationship often remains fairly static if you rely on royalties alone. Extended revenue channels, from coaching to exclusive retreats, allow your audience to engage more intimately with your content. They don't just read your advice; they experience it interactively, *and* they pay a premium for that direct experience. Cool, isn't it?!

Big Idea #2: Consulting and Coaching: Translating Ideas into Action

Consulting and coaching are two of the most common pathways entrepreneurs take after publication. If your book offers proven strategies, frameworks, or unique perspectives, it's likely that a subset of your readership craves deeper, more personalized guidance.

1. One-on-One Coaching

a. How It Works

You position yourself as a personal or executive coach, offering individual sessions that dive deeper into the methodology you discuss in your book. Whether you're an expert in leadership, operations management, marketing, or mindset mastery, your published book acts as an authoritative calling card.

b. Pricing and Structure

• **Hourly Rates vs. Package Deals:** Some coaches charge per session (often at a higher hourly rate) while others sell multi-month packages.

• **Client Onboarding:** A streamlined onboarding process, possibly via many available online software (SaaS), helps capture leads, schedule sessions, and manage billing.

• **Scaling with Group Coaching:** If your demand grows, group coaching can multiply income. For example, group sessions can be 25–50% less than your individual rate while you still earn more per hour overall.

c. Pros

- Direct, relationship-based income.
- Immediate market feedback (coaching conversations often reveal new pain points and opportunities).
- Builds testimonial-worthy success stories, which can feed back into your brand.

d. Cons

- Time-intensive; your earning potential is somewhat capped by how many clients you can personally handle.
- Requires strong interpersonal and communication skills—writing ability alone won't suffice.

2. Business Consulting

a. Consulting vs. Coaching

While coaching focuses on guiding individuals to solutions via introspection, consulting typically involves offering expert advice and possibly rolling up your sleeves to implement processes within a client's company. For many entrepreneurs, this could be a great marketing strategy to acquire high-paying clients to their business.

b. Securing Consulting Gigs

- **Case Studies & Portfolio:** Prospective clients want tangible proof you can deliver. Documenting any transformations your ideas facilitated—like a startup that doubled revenue after applying your book's framework—will be key.
- **Network Leveraging:** Your book likely expanded your professional contacts (as discussed in previous chapters). These relationships can become a direct referral pipeline for consulting opportunities.

c. Pricing Models

- **Project-based fees:** Flat rates for specific deliverables, e.g., a marketing audit or a six-week operational overhaul.
- **Retainer:** An ongoing monthly fee for consistent advisory support.
- **Equity Stakes:** For startups or small businesses, you might consider equity in exchange for lower fees, though this raises risk and complexity.

Big Idea #3: Paid Speaking: Beyond the Podium

For many authors, speaking engagements are the most glamorous and high-profile of post-publication opportunities. It's most logical next step. These chances can also be among the most lucrative, especially if your entrepreneurial focus resonates with major industry events.

1. Building Your Speaker Platform

a. Speaker Reel and Profile

A professional speaker reel—a short video capturing your on-stage presence—can be invaluable for securing paid gigs. In lieu of a reel, testimonial videos from your first few speaking appearances can also work wonders.

b. Conference and Event Strategy

- **Start Local**: Contact local business associations, chambers of commerce, or meetup groups to refine your speech.
- **Leverage Social Media**: Platforms like LinkedIn enable you to announce your speaking availability and share snippets from past events.
- **Apply to Speak**: Large conferences often open a call for speakers. An effective pitch references your book's topic and offers fresh insights or workshop-style interactions.

2. Types of Speaking Opportunities

- **Keynotes**: Typically, the main highlight of a conference. Keynotes can command high fees, from a few thousand to tens of thousands of dollars, depending on your profile and the event budget.
- **Breakout Sessions/Workshops**: More interactive formats where you dive deep into hands-on activities relevant to your book's content.
- **Corporate Off-Sites or Retreats**: Companies often invite authors to energize or educate their teams, paying premium rates for engaging, brand-relevant sessions.

3. Monetizing Speaking: Fees, Books, and Upsells

- **Speaking Fees**: Depending on your industry and personal brand, fees can range from $1,000 for small-scale events to $20,000+ for major conferences.

• **On-Site Book Sales**: If the event doesn't purchase books in bulk for attendees, you may still sell copies post-session at a signing table, earning direct profit and forging personal connections.

• **Upselling Consulting or Courses**: A speaking engagement can be the stepping-stone to follow-up business. Attendees who resonate with your talk might later hire you for consulting or join your coaching program.

Big Idea #4: Creating Digital Products: Courses, Webinars, and Membership

When it comes to scaling your expertise beyond the written page, digital products stand as a formidable option. Their potential lies in **asynchronous accessibility**—people can learn from you 24/7, anywhere in the world, without the scheduling constraints of in-person services.

1. Online Courses

a. Content Conversion

Take the major lessons or frameworks in your book and expand them into step-by-step training modules. For instance, if your book is about mastering e-commerce logistics, your online course could feature videos showing real warehouse management systems, interactive quizzes, and templates for cost optimization.

b. Platform Selection

• **Standalone Course Platforms**: Think Teachable, Thinkific, Kajabi, etc.

• **Marketplace Platforms**: Sites like Udemy or Skillshare can offer built-in traffic but typically require lower price points.

c. Pricing

• Basic self-paced courses might range from $49 to $299.

• Premium, comprehensive courses with personalized feedback and group coaching components can cost $500 to $2,000+. Stardom's Book Writing Course sells for $1000 retail.

d. Marketing Your Course

- **Lead Magnets**: Offer a downloadable PDF (e.g., a workbook excerpted from your book) in exchange for email addresses.
- **Email Automations**: Nurture leads through a series of automated emails, culminating in a pitch for the course (eg. Mailerlite, Aweber, Constant Contact, etc.)
- **Cross-Promotion**: Announce and link to the course in your book's introduction or conclusion, or within social media posts that reference the book.

2. Webinars and Live Events

a. Why Webinars?

Webinars provide a more personal connection than purely self-paced courses. They also serve as a superb funnel to higher-priced offers. You might deliver free or low-cost webinars on topics aligned with your book, then pitch a more comprehensive product or service at the end.

b. "Perfect" Webinar Structure

- **Introduction**: Quick personal backstory and a reference to your book's major theme.
- **Teaching Segment:** Provide valuable lessons or frameworks that address a specific pain point from your book.
- **Interactive Element:** Polls, Q&A, or breakout rooms (if using advanced webinar software).
- **Closing** Offer: A direct invitation to enroll in your larger course, coaching program, or workshop.

"Resilience is the key to success. So, don't be afraid to take risks and learn from your mistakes."

> **Webinar Conversion Statistics for Authors**[1,2,3]
>
> Hosting educational webinars can be a powerful strategy for authors promoting premium services. Here are key industry statistics:
>
> • **Registration Rate:** Up to **51%** of visitors register for a webinar.
>
> • **Attendance Rate:** Around **50%** of registrants actually attend.
>
> • **Lead Conversion: 20%–40%** of attendees become qualified leads.
>
> • **Sales Conversion:** Industry averages range from **1.2%** (finance) to **2.5%** (biotech).
>
> Success depends on content quality, audience engagement, and follow-up strategies. Authors who provide valuable insights and strong calls to action can improve conversions.

3. Membership or Subscription Models

a. Recurring Revenue

A membership site that delivers monthly content, group calls, or new resource releases can be a lucrative add-on. For example, entrepreneurs who wrote about leadership might create a membership community where each month they release a new leadership toolkit, a video Q&A, and host a group coaching call.

b. Community Building

Beyond the financial upside, these memberships build a sense of loyalty and belonging around your brand. Readers become part of a tribe where they can ask questions, collaborate, and celebrate wins—all guided by your overarching methods or philosophies from the book.

---

1. GetContrast. 2024. "Webinar Statistics: Benchmarks and Insights." GetContrast. https://www.getcontrast.io/learn/webinar-statistics.

2. Hubilo. 2024. "Webinar Marketing Statistics & Benchmarks." Hubilo. https://www.hubilo.com/blog/webinar-marketing-statistics-benchmarks.

3. DemandSage. 2024. "Webinar Statistics: Key Insights & Trends." DemandSage. https://www.demandsage.com/webinar-statistics

c. Pricing and Tiered Access

• Basic membership tiers might start at $19 to $49 a month, offering core content.

• **Premium** tiers, at $99 to $299+ a month, could include private coaching calls or exclusive networking events. Eg. StardomCircle.com – my premium mastermind membership for leaders.

Big Idea #5: Corporate Partnerships, Sponsorships, and Licensing

Some of the most lucrative and scalable monetization avenues come from partnering with larger organizations. These can extend beyond speaking to integrated programs or even licensing your intellectual property.

1. Corporate Training & Workshops

a. Why Corporations Need You

Companies often have training budgets for leadership development, innovation, mental wellness, or specialized skill-building. If your book addresses a critical challenge—like digital transformation or organizational culture—businesses may hire you to run half-day or full-day workshops for their teams.

b. Packaging Your Workshop

• **Participant Workbooks**: Adapt relevant chapters into interactive workbook formats.

• **Case Studies**: Incorporate examples from your own entrepreneurial journey that map onto corporate experiences.

• **Follow-Up Resources**: Offer a short e-guide or webinar series for employees who want to continue learning.

c. Fee Structures

• **Daily Rate**: Ranges widely based on your expertise and the company size; from $2,000/day to $15,000+/day.

• **Per-Attendee Licensing**: Corporate clients may license your training material for a set number of participants.

2. Brand Sponsorship and Cross-Promotions

If your book targets a specific audience—like "Entrepreneurial Moms" or "Sustainable Small Businesses"—you can sometimes team up with brands eager to reach that group. You might collaborate on specialized events, co-branded content, or promotional campaigns.

Potential Sponsorships

• **Sponsored Digital Summits**: You invite multiple speakers around your book's theme, and a brand sponsors the event in exchange for visibility.

• **Joint Giveaways**: The brand provides a free product or service, and you offer your book or mini-course to their audience.

• **Exclusive Chapters or Excerpts**: A brand may pay to feature a special chapter focusing on how their solution aligns with your principles, as long as it fits ethically and organically with your book's message.

3. Licensing Your Book's Intellectual Property

a. Courseware Licensing

If your book has a proven methodology, educational institutions or training companies may license your content to incorporate into their official curricula. This approach can be especially relevant if your book addresses professional development, leadership, or entrepreneurial strategy.

b. International Licensing & Translations

Exploring foreign-language markets can significantly expand your reach—and your income. You might arrange a licensing deal with an international publisher who translates and distributes your book abroad. Along with royalties on each sale, you can secure additional fees for associated training materials.

Big Idea #6: Building a Personalized Ecosystem: Masterminds, Live Events, and Retreats

When your book strikes a chord, some readers will want to go far deeper, forging long-term relationships with you and others who share their mindset. This is where masterminds, retreats, and niche events shine.

1. Mastermind Programs

a. What is a Mastermind?

A mastermind typically involves a small group of motivated individuals who commit to meeting regularly (virtually or in person) under the guidance of a facilitator (you). The concept is that collectively, the group's intelligence, support, and accountability produce exponential personal and professional growth.

b. Designing Your Mastermind

- **Duration**: 3, 6, or 12 months are common formats.
- **Group Size**: Usually between 5 and 15 members to maintain intimacy and effective feedback.
- **Curriculum**: The backbone of the mastermind is often the major themes from your book—expanded with exercises, group discussions, and hot-seat sessions.

c. Pricing

Masterminds can run anywhere from $1,000 for a 3-month group to tens of thousands of dollars for elite, extended programs. The premium is justified by the high-touch environment and transformative experiences.

2. Exclusive Retreats or Live Intensives

For entrepreneurs or professionals wanting an immersive experience, consider hosting retreats that revolve around your book's core principles—be that leadership, growth hacking, wellness, or creativity.

a. Retreat Structure

- **Venue Selection**: Choose a setting aligned with your brand ethos (e.g., a countryside villa for a mindfulness-oriented book or a bustling urban environment for an innovation-focused event).
- **Agenda:** Mix workshops, networking sessions, guest speakers (if relevant), personal reflection time, and on-the-spot coaching.
- **Pricing:** Premium retreats can cost participants $2,000 to $10,000+ depending on the location, duration, and included amenities.

b. Benefits

- Deep rapport with your audience, reinforcing loyalty and word-of-mouth marketing.
- Potential for robust upsells (participants might join long-term coaching or licensing deals after a transformative weekend).

Big Idea #7: Revenue Funnel Key Insights

To effectively manage and automate these various streams, it's helpful to conceptualize your offerings as part of a strategic funnel. Each tier addresses different audience segments:

1. Free Content / Low-Cost Entry
- Readers purchase your book or sign up for a free webinar.
- Purpose: Attract and nurture wide awareness.

2. Mid-Tier Offer
- Online courses, group coaching programs, or workshops priced moderately.
- Purpose: Generate a sustainable, predictable income stream from engaged fans.

3. Premium, High-Touch Packages
- One-on-one consulting, corporate licenses, private masterminds, or retreats.
- Purpose: Provide your most personalized services at a premium cost.

Big Idea #8: Sustainable Monetization – Mindset Shift

1. Moving from "Author" to "Authority"

Royalties alone often place the book and its sales front and center. But once you see yourself as a problem-solver, advisor, and educator, you'll naturally transition into exploring ways to monetize that authority. This shift is as much about self-perception as it is about business strategy.

2. Balancing Passion with Profit

While it's empowering to earn from your book, authenticity remains critical. Ensure every new endeavor aligns with the book's message and with your core entrepreneurial values. Chasing misaligned revenue can dilute your brand and leave readers feeling disillusioned.

3. Continuous Improvement

Monitor feedback from your digital products, speaking audiences, and corporate clients. Adapt your frameworks, revisit your content, and consider releasing updated editions or new companion resources to meet evolving market needs.

The Power of Regular Content Updates in Sustaining Author Revenue in the Long Run [4]

• **Increased Engagement & Discoverability:** A 2023 study found that while only 38% of bloggers update older content, 34% reported strong results from doing so. This suggests that updated content retains visibility and relevance, leading to sustained traffic and potential revenue.

• **Sales & Business Growth:** A qualitative study on online marketing strategies found that businesses implementing content updates saw increased sales and long-term growth. This principle applies to authors, whose refreshed editions attract new and returning readers.

• **Sustained Revenue Over 2–3 Years:** While direct long-term studies on authors remain limited, data from online marketing and blogging trends indicate that consistent content updates can drive sustained revenue growth over multiple years post-publication.

Authors who strategically update their content maintain audience engagement, boost discoverability, and sustain revenue growth over time.

---

4. OptinMonster, *Blogging Statistics: Key Data and Trends for 2023*, 2023, https://optinmonster.com/blogging-statistics. Walden University, *Implementing Effective Online Marketing Strategies for Small Retail Businesses*, Walden Dissertations and Doctoral Studies, 2023, https://scholarworks.waldenu.edu/cgi/viewcontent.cgi?article=7175&context=dissertations.

Big Idea #9: Avoiding Pitfalls – 4 Big Mistakes

1. Overextending Too Quickly: Each new initiative—coaching, courses, events—requires time and resources. Pace your expansions so you can maintain quality.

2. Underpricing Premium Offers: While you might be tempted to keep prices low to attract clients, undervaluing your expertise can lead to burnout and hamper your perceived authority.

3. Poor Promotion of New Ventures: Creating these offerings is only half the battle. You need consistent promotion across social media, email newsletters, and speaking engagements to ensure traction.

4. Mismatched Partnerships: When aligning with sponsors or corporations, ensure synergy in brand values and messaging. A wrong match can damage your credibility with readers.

Big Idea #10: Action Steps: Your Monetization Roadmap

Here are the steps to help you lay out a personalized strategy for monetizing your book beyond royalties. Use them as a checklist or reference guide:

1. Audit Your Content
- Identify the most valuable insights in your book. Which sections or chapters resonate most deeply with readers?
- Consider potential expansions: exercises, templates, deeper case studies.

2. Evaluate Your Audience
- Who are your most engaged readers or followers?
- What are the biggest challenges they face that extend beyond your book?

3. Select Your Flagship Offer
- Choose a single next step—perhaps an online course, coaching, or a mastermind—that you can realistically develop and market in the next 3–6 months.

4. Create a Timeline

• Design backward from your launch date. Include time for content creation, marketing asset development, beta testing, and final polishing.

5. Test the Market

• Conduct a webinar or poll your existing mailing list to gauge interest.

• Offer early-bird pricing for those willing to provide testimonials or feedback.

6. Leverage Existing Platforms

• Share news about your new offer in the concluding pages of your book.

• Mention the service on podcasts or interviews that reference your book.

7. Refine and Scale

• Gather feedback, monitor key metrics, and revise as needed.

• If the offer succeeds, expand into additional streams or higher-priced tiers, possibly incorporating advanced content or more personalized services.

From One-Time Royalty Checks to Lasting Impact

Royalties may be the initial financial reward for the intellectual labor of writing your book, but they are truly just **the beginning**. As an entrepreneur, you already understand the power of leveraging assets. Your manuscript is an asset—a reservoir of expertise, stories, and actionable advice—that can empower people on far deeper levels than passive reading alone.

By branching into consulting, coaching, speaking, digital products, corporate partnerships, licensing, and community-based programs, you transform your book into a **central pillar** for an entire ecosystem of offerings. Each step you take beyond royalties will not only enhance your revenue but also deepen your connection to your audience, amplify your reach, and open new avenues for professional and personal growth. So, don't let your book's potential remain confined to bookstore shelves—literal or digital. Tap into these strategies, and you'll soon discover that authorship is far more than a single financial moment. It's a renewable resource for ongoing income and enduring impact, fueling both your entrepreneurial journey and the readers who've trusted in your vision.

"Life is a journey, and while it's important to stay focused on your goals, don't forget to take the time to appreciate the little things that make life worth living."

> **Key Takeaways**
>
> - **Consulting & Coaching**: Translate the core insights from your book into high-touch advisory services that offer personalized guidance and generate robust income.
>
> - **Paid Speaking Engagements**: Leverage your author credibility to secure keynotes, breakout sessions, and corporate retreats, often at premium rates.
>
> - **Digital Products**: Develop online courses, membership communities, or webinars that scale your reach and supplement passive income.
>
> - **Corporate Partnerships & Licensing**: Provide customized workshops or license your methods for broader corporate training, unlocking large-scale revenue.
>
> - **Community-Building Ventures**: Consider masterminds, retreats, and live events to foster deep, ongoing relationships with your most committed readers.
>
> - **Think Funnel**: Organize your offerings into a strategic pathway—from low-cost entry points to premium services—ensuring continuous engagement and revenue growth.

10

HOW TO ACHIEVE THIS DREAM OUTCOME

"You can, you should, and if you're brave enough to start, you will."
—**Stephen King**

Did you know 92% of people want to write a book, but less than 1% actually do!

Let me introduce a true trailblazer, Srini Rajam, the brilliant mind behind Ittiam Systems (Chairman and CEO). With a vision to lead the charge of Indian technology products on the global stage, Srini and his dynamic team embarked on an incredible journey. Now, here's the twist – Srini, a seasoned expert in his field, had already guided others to success. Yet, when it came to crafting his own book, he realized the power of seeking professional guidance.

Srini Rajam, a luminary in the tech realm, decided to approach (our) publishing house and team up with a professional coach. Think about it – this guy has not only excelled in his field but has guided others under his leadership to achieve their best. So, what prompted him to collaborate with a coach for his own book? Well, it's simple – the process of writing a book is a whole different ball game, and Srini recognized the value of having a guiding hand.

Together with a group of seasoned professionals, Srini co-founded Ittiam Systems. This visionary initiative encapsulates the collective dreams of six leaders, each with a wealth of global experience in designing cutting-edge products. Their mission? To spearhead a new era of Indian technology marvels that shine brightly on the world stage.

Diving into his inspiring journey of writing *"Steering the Ship to the Shore: Guide for Founders Navigating Startup Waters"*—and how his partnership with me, Raam Anand, helped turn his vision into a powerful, game-changing reality.

You see, Srini Rajam, a tech industry veteran and former CEO of Texas Instruments, had a treasure trove of knowledge and stories from his extensive career. But here's the catch – he needed to distill all that wisdom into a book that would captivate not just tech-savvy folks but a broader audience, too.

That's where I sailed in. Right from the get-go, I helped Srini chart the course. We tackled the massive task of structuring the book together. Think of it like crafting a map that guides readers through the tumultuous waters of startup life. We meticulously planned where stories, insights, and examples would fit perfectly to create a compelling journey.

As Srini penned down his thoughts, I was his compass. With every chapter, I provided invaluable feedback that turned raw ideas into polished prose. My team and I fine-tuned sentences, juggled words, and ensured that the book's tone stayed engaging while still delivering Srini's profound message loud and clear.

But wait, there's more. When Srini faced choppy writing waters or encountered moments of self-doubt (which, let's be honest, every writer does), I was there with a lifebuoy of motivation. I kept Srini's eyes on the prize, reminding him why he embarked on this literary voyage in the first place.

And then, the moment arrived – the manuscript was ready. But hey, publishing? It's like sailing into uncharted territories. With my industry knowledge, I became Srini's navigation system. I steered Srini through the bewildering sea of publishing options and shared savvy marketing strategies that would ensure their book's success.

In 2023, *"Steering the Ship to the Shore"* hit the shelves, and guess what? It didn't just make a splash – it was a full-blown tidal wave. Readers across the globe hailed it as a game-changer, praising its engaging writing and powerful insights.

And who does Srini credit for this success? You guessed it – his coach, Raam Anand (yay!). This journey exemplifies how a coach's guidance can elevate a vision from a mere concept to a tangible, impactful masterpiece. It's a testament to the transformative power of having a coach by your side every step of the way.

WHY YOU SHOULD HIRE A PUBLISHING COACH

Working with a coach is a journey towards success. They play a crucial role in creating a clear path with achievable milestones. Their guidance in developing a system for writing and publishing a book, regular evaluation of your progress, and making necessary adjustments all contribute to a sense of being guided and supported. A coach can also provide valuable assistance in organizing and developing a book or book proposal, offer useful plans and tools to expedite the book's launch, expand the author's platform, and craft compelling and comprehensive promotional plans for the book.

That said, choosing a coach is not an easy task. You will have to consider many things. To help you, here are seven critical factors to consider when hiring ANY coach:

- **Values Alignment:**

  Are your values aligned with the coach's? For example, you might be a fun-loving, upbeat, and laid-back person, and your coach is more like an old-school drillmaster. In this situation, you might struggle to understand and apply the practices and strategies they impart to you. For instance, if you value creativity and your coach is more focused on structure, it could lead to a clash of perspectives. While this may be an extreme example, you should be aware that even the slightest hint of incompatibility between your values and your coaches can cause this process of writing your book to be knocked askew.

- **Verifiable Results:**

Have they created or produced the same results you want to manifest, or do they 'just teach this stuff' from reading books on those topics? Would it not be better to learn from those people who have traveled on the same path that you now want to traverse? Is it not better to learn from those who can walk their talk and who have 'been there done that'?

Your coach should be more than just a guide. They should be a role model, inspiring you with their success and track record of making a positive difference in the world. Their success should serve as a source of inspiration, motivating you to reach the same heights. This emphasis on their role as a role model should leave you feeling inspired and motivated.

Another point to note here is that your coach should be successful in terms of what you think success is. After all, success is relative and unique to every individual.

- **Experience/Education:**

When choosing a coach, it's crucial to consider their qualifications and experience. Are they truly equipped to help you succeed with education and experience that's been tested in the marketplace? Or are they simply regurgitating content they've learned from others? This emphasis on their experience and education should reassure you and instill confidence in your choice.

If I were to look for an expert to learn from, I would always choose the person who has worked in the particular field and who will, therefore, have valuable and viable insights to share. So, if you are looking to hire the services of a coach to help publish your book, you should look for someone who has excelled in all three areas—reading (someone who reads a lot of books), writing (who has already written their own books), and publishing (who has published other peoples' books).

"Life is a balance between giving and taking, so don't be afraid to ask for help when you need it while also lending a helping hand when possible"

- **Satisfied Clients:**

  Client satisfaction matters; who are the coach's clients? Are they satisfied with the results? Check their testimonials and reviews. It's crucial to gather feedback before committing. This will give you a clear picture of the coach's effectiveness and help you make an informed decision. Knowing that the coach has a track record of satisfied clients can give you confidence in your choice.

- **Program Content:**

  Consider the methods your coach plans to use. Will you enjoy implementing their strategies? Will you find their process fun and authentic? It's not just about the end result but also about the journey. It's important to make an informed decision. Working with a coach you don't vibe with can compromise the quality of your book. So, ensure you're comfortable with their methods and that you'll enjoy the coaching process.

- **Facing Challenges Head-On:**

  Enquire if your prospective coach or mentor has dealt with their share of challenges. These need not have been in the same field as yours, but make sure your coach has been where you are now. If your mentor/coach has had it easy, you might have difficulty bonding with them. Why is this important? Well, a coach who has gone through life hurdles will help you see the world as it is and prepare you for all sorts of challenges life might throw at you.

> - **Learning Structure:**
> Analyze and review the methods your coach uses. Are you being benefited? Are his/her teachings and ways aiding you in reaching your goal? Having said that, do not rush and make a hasty decision. Some things take time.
>
> So, after a month or two of coaching, take the time to review your progress. If you feel that the coaching relationship isn't working for you, it's okay to seek a different coach. This review process empowers you to make the best decision for your writing journey. I encourage you to use these pointers as a checklist to evaluate your options and choose a coach who aligns with your needs.

Publishing Choices

In the dynamic landscape of publishing choices, authors have a myriad of avenues to embark upon, each catering to distinct aspirations and available means. Exploring the wide spectrum of publishing choices and adeptly navigating the path that aligns seamlessly with your unique goals and resources has become an intricate art. Unlike earlier days, where a single publishing route was the only option, today's authors are presented with an enriching array of possibilities. Here are three major forms of publishing, each offering its own blend of advantages and considerations:

- Traditional publishing (Where art meets establishment)
- Self-publishing (Crafting your narrative your way)
- Hybrid publishing (Striking the balance)

Hybrid publishing emerges as an enchanting crossroads where the worlds of traditional and self-publishing harmoniously converge. Hybrid publishing, which sits somewhere between traditional and self-publishing, provides a mix of professional services while allowing authors to keep more control. This avenue provides advantages akin to traditional publishing while affording flexibility, coaching, and a more participatory role in the process. However, costs can be moderate, and the quality of support may vary. Authors who yearn for a harmonious blend of professional guidance and creative influence find hybrid publishing an appealing choice.

At Stardom Books, we embrace this hybrid publishing model, orchestrating a harmonious synergy between the author's influence and the publishing house's guidance. This unique approach transforms the author-publisher relationship into a genuine partnership that nurtures creativity while ensuring a polished and market-savvy final product.

Stardom Books' unique hybrid publishing technique smoothly merges the author's creative vision with the expertise of a publishing business. Our editors edit the content, and the sales team handles the marketing. Hybrid publishing is the best of both worlds. This dynamic collaboration ushered in a new age in book publishing by allowing for a collaborative partnership that blends the capabilities of both traditional publishing and self-publishing methods.

1. Creative Control: Unlike traditional publishing, hybrid publishing empowers authors to maintain their creative vision. There are no rigid norms, allowing authors to shape their work authentically and confidently.

2. Professional Support: Authors benefit from the editors' professional insights while maintaining control over their content. This collaboration fosters a respectful exchange of ideas and enhances the quality of the work, making authors feel valued and respected.

3. Focus on Craft: Hybrid publishing offers the autonomy of self-publishing but relieves authors from the complexities of marketing and publishing logistics. This lets authors concentrate on writing, knowing that experts handle the essential aspects, making them feel relieved and focused.

4. Partnership Approach: Hybrid publishers view authors as partners rather than clients. This relationship often results in higher and more frequent royalty payouts compared to traditional publishers.

5. Honoring Individuality: The editing style in hybrid publishing respects and preserves the author's unique voice, ensuring that their personality resonates through the pages.

6. Flexibility: Hybrid publishing adapts to industry changes, providing the flexibility to evolve with market trends.

7. Mentorship: Authors receive guidance from mentors throughout the intricate publishing journey, enhancing their experience and success.

Even though the pros outweigh the cons, here's a clearer picture.

The only hitch of hybrid publishing, if you feel so, are:

1. Initial Financial Investment: Unlike self-publishing, hybrid publishing requires an upfront financial commitment. Authors invest in the professional presentation and refinement of their work.

2. Brand Recognition: Hybrid publishing may not yet have the same name or brand recognition as traditional publishing houses. However, the benefits often outweigh this 'not-so-important' difference.

3. Perceived Prestige: Some authors mistakenly believe traditional publishing is inherently more prestigious. However, the notable successes achieved through hybrid publishing models have debunked this myth.

The privilege of professional support and creative agency comes with a price. It's essential to research hybrid publishers diligently to ensure they align with the author's aspirations. Hybrid publishing offers a bridge between artistic freedom and professional guidance, ensuring authors retain their creative essence while receiving expert support. This approach allows authors to leverage their expertise while ensuring their books are professionally polished and well-marketed.

WHY CHOOSE HYBRID PUBLISHING WITH STARDOM BOOKS?

Stardom Books offers the **best of both worlds—creative freedom** and **professional guidance**. Authors can make key decisions about their books while benefiting from the expertise of seasoned professionals.

Hybrid publishing is **flexible**, adapting to your specific goals, whether it's achieving broad readership, maintaining control over your content, or optimizing financial returns. It requires a moderate investment, balancing cost and quality.

It combines the **strengths** of traditional and self-publishing, allowing authors to reach **niche audiences** and **broader markets** effectively.

Professional marketing strategies are employed to ensure your book gets the visibility it deserves.

Access to expert editors, designers, and marketers ensures your book meets **high standards**. This **professional touch enhances** the overall **quality** and **marketability** of your book.

The success of authors like Srini Rajam highlights the efficacy of hybrid publishing. By blending personal effort with professional support, hybrid publishing can elevate one's work and amplify one's message.

Choosing the right publishing path is crucial for your book's success. Stardom Books offers a balanced approach that can meet diverse author needs. It provides professional support while allowing creative control, making it an ideal choice for many authors. By evaluating your goals, assessing your resources, understanding your audience, and seeking professional guidance, you can make an informed decision that aligns with your literary aspirations and enhances your book's impact.

At Stardom Books, we offer a holistic approach to publishing, ensuring that every aspect of your book journey is covered. Our services encompass planning, writing, finishing, publishing, marketing, and leveraging your book for maximum impact. We pride ourselves on transforming the publishing experience and helping authors become thought leaders and influencers.

1. Planning: Meticulous Book Outline Creation

Like skilled architects, our highly trained publishing advisors meticulously craft a detailed outline for your book, ensuring you have 100% clarity on your project from the start. This eliminates surprises later on and sets a solid foundation for your book's success.

2. Writing: Professional Writing Assistance

Our trained team collaborates with you to write your book using proven resources, structures, frameworks, techniques, and tactics. This process saves you time and frustration, ensuring a smooth writing experience and a high-quality manuscript.

3. Finishing: Comprehensive Editing and Formatting

Your rough manuscript is transformed into a polished piece of art through several rounds of editing, formatting, proofreading, and mockups. We ensure that you will be proud to present your book to the world.

4. Publishing: Global Publishing and Distribution

Stardom Books publishes your book globally in both digital (eBook) and paperback (print) editions, distributing it to a massive network of bookstores, libraries, and distribution platforms. This ensures your book reaches readers worldwide quickly and efficiently.

5. Leveraging: Author Coaching and Consulting

We provide incredible coaching, consulting, and support to help you maximize your new identity as an author. Our goal is to help you achieve the maximum return on investment (ROI) and elevate your status as a thought leader.

Partnership and Ownership

With Stardom Books, you always retain the copyrights and intellectual property of your book. We see our relationship with authors as a partnership, ensuring you get the best value for your investment. Unlike other services that cut corners, we prioritize quality and your reputation, making sure your book reflects the best of your identity and expertise.

Choosing Stardom Books means opting for a comprehensive, supportive, and professional publishing experience that elevates you as an author and thought leader.

Example: Elizabeth Gilbert's "Eat, Pray, Love"

I bet you have come across, or maybe even seen, the movie *"Eat, Pray, Love."* The book, authored by an American journalist, was adapted into a live motion film starring none other than Julia Roberts. But did you know that the book remained on The New York Times Best Seller list for 187 weeks? Let me share an inspiring story about the renowned author Elizabeth Gilbert and how she overcame her struggles with writing thanks to the invaluable guidance of her writing coach, Dinty W. Moore.

Before achieving tremendous success with her bestselling memoir *"Eat, Pray, Love,"* Gilbert had already put forth her works - a collection of short stories and a novel. Despite her talent, these previous books did not receive the recognition she had hoped for, leaving her feeling disheartened and unsure of her abilities.

Amid a personal crisis, Gilbert embarked on a transformative journey, traveling to different parts of the world to heal and search for her life's purpose. It was during this time that she found solace in writing, pouring her emotions and experiences into the pages of her new project, *"Eat, Pray, Love."*

Recognizing the need for guidance and support to shape her raw material into a captivating narrative, Gilbert sought the mentorship of Dinty W. Moore. Moore, an accomplished author himself, proved to be a pivotal figure in her writing journey. With his profound understanding of storytelling and writing techniques, Moore helped Gilbert weave her personal experiences into a relatable and emotionally authentic tale.

Under Moore's expert tutelage, Gilbert learned to focus on her own voice and the emotional truth in her writing. This emphasis on authenticity added a powerful dimension to her memoir, making it resonate deeply with readers from all walks of life.

The impact of Moore's coaching became evident when *"Eat, Pray, Love"* soared to international acclaim. The book found its place on the New York Times Best Seller list, captivating readers around the globe with its profound message of self-discovery and healing.

Gilbert's triumphant journey didn't end there. The success of *"Eat, Pray, Love"* extended to Hollywood, where the memoir was adapted into a compelling feature film, reaching an even wider audience.

Through her collaboration with Dinty W. Moore, Gilbert not only discovered her own writing prowess but also unlocked the power of vulnerability and honesty in storytelling. Her story serves as a testament to the transformative impact of having a dedicated writing coach, someone who can provide valuable insights, encouragement, and the tools needed to bring out the best in a writer's work.

So, if you ever find yourself struggling with your writing or facing uncertainty in your creative journey, remember Elizabeth Gilbert's experience. Seek out a mentor or writing coach who can help you uncover your authentic voice, and like her, you may discover a path to success that you never thought possible.

Just like tackling any other big challenge, writing a book is a pretty major milestone. So, having a good coach to help you along the way can be a game-changer when it comes to setting clear goals for your book. A coach will be your wing-person, helping you navigate through all the twists and turns of book writing and making sure you keep sight of that result you're aiming for.

You know what's cool? Even the big shots of the world, those high achievers, they've got coaches, too. And get this – they've got coaches for all sorts of stuff like fitness, business, meditation, spirituality, money matters, high performance, parenting, communicating the right way, voice training, managing like a boss, and even helping up their fashion game. It just goes to show how having a coach is like having a secret weapon to supercharge all kinds of areas in life!

In the dynamic realm of publishing and writing, aspiring authors and seasoned writers frequently turn to the expertise of publishing and writing coaches. These professionals serve as compasses, guiding individuals through the intricate waters of the publishing industry and helping them elevate their writing prowess.

A publishing coach is akin to a wise mentor, guiding writers through the entire journey of developing a manuscript. Their role is multifaceted, encompassing the refinement of ideas, the artful structuring of content, and the meticulous polishing of prose to meet the exacting standards of the industry. A writing coach is your personal wordsmith guru. They focus on enhancing an author's writing skills holistically. Think style, grammar, and the intricate craft of storytelling – these are the elements they delve into, ensuring that the content weaves its magic on readers.

The allure of engaging with a publishing and writing coach is particularly beneficial for those who are newly entering the field or aiming to ascend to new heights. The coaches are akin to living encyclopedias of industry knowledge, well-versed in the ebbs and flows of trends and the ever-changing desires of the market.

Through collaborative efforts with a coach, authors and writers can unearth the intricacies of book publication or sharpen their writer's toolkit. The guidance bestowed by these skilled mentors exponentially boosts the prospects of success in an arena where competition is fierce.

From refining the nuances of a manuscript to sculpting captivating narratives that linger in readers' minds, the decision to enlist a publishing or writing coach is a doorway to indispensable support on the journey toward realizing literary ambitions. It's a step that holds the promise of transforming aspiring writers into accomplished authors and taking seasoned wordsmiths to dazzling new heights.

Taking a structured approach

Transitioning from being unnoticed to becoming an influential authority is an essential part of a comprehensive roadmap called the Authority Influencer Roadmap. Many experts, entrepreneurs, specialists, professionals, and thought leaders invest significant time in mastering their skills but fail to receive the recognition they deserve. As a result, they remain unseen, under-recognized, and relatively unknown in their fields. Let's get straight to the point. The Authority Influencer Roadmap consists of three stages: Plan, Build, and Launch. By following this roadmap, you can increase your influence, establish authority, enhance your reputation, strengthen your personal brand, and ultimately become an influencer in your niche. Here's how you can do it:

> **PLAN:** In the first phase, you will undertake three crucial steps. These steps include Getting in the Game, identifying your Circle of Influence, and Crafting Your Core Message. This phase focuses on gaining clarity about your current situation, pinpointing the specific audience you aim to reach, and developing a core message that resonates with that audience. It's about aligning your goals with the goals, problems, and aspirations of your audience.

> **BUILD:** The second phase builds upon the clarity gained in Phase 1. This phase involves creating your influence model, outlining your core message, and producing highly engaging and compelling content in various formats. You will also learn how to repurpose and summarize your content, create social and marketing assets, and build your email list. These efforts will help you spread your message and establish a strong presence in the industry.

> **LAUNCH:** The third phase is the most exciting one. It begins with the creation and publication of your own book. Writing a book is a powerful strategy to position yourself as a top influencer and authority in your industry. It allows you to reach your specific audience and make a significant impact. As you start making this impact, your influence will grow, fueling your overall growth and effectiveness.

"The Authority Influencer Roadmap" is a potent tool, but it requires you to understand and navigate each phase of the nine-step process. Startup founders often struggle with not knowing where or how to start writing a book, especially if they have never done it before. A structured approach tailored for you can be immensely helpful. Let me outline a nine-step process from the Authority Influencer Roadmap that can address this issue:

1. Define your purpose: Clearly articulate why you want to write a book, aligning it with your personal and professional goals. Your purpose will guide you throughout the writing journey.

2. Identify your audience: Define your target readers. Understanding their needs, interests, and challenges is crucial. This knowledge will help you craft a book that resonates with them.

3. Establish your key message: Outline the core message or central theme of your book. This should be the key idea you want readers to take away. For example, this book we are creating right now is for startup founders and focuses on how they can navigate the process of writing a book and determine if it is the right choice for them.

4. Create a content map or outline: Develop a broad structure for your book. Include key topics or ideas that you want to cover, organizing them logically. Our publishing advisors at Stardom Books can assist in creating the entire book outline for you.

5. Create your first draft: Once your outline is complete, start writing your first draft. Alternatively, you can have a writer work on it based on the detailed outline you prepared. At this stage, don't worry about perfecting language or grammar; focus on getting your thoughts down on paper.

6. Revise and refine: After completing the final draft, begin revising and refining it. Pay attention to improving language, filling content gaps, and ensuring flow and coherence. If you're working with a publishing team like Stardom Books, their editorial team will handle this step.

7. Prepare for publication: Once your manuscript is ready, edited, and print-ready, begin preparing for publishing. This involves professional editing by a group of editors or publishing experts. Formatting and designing a cover that aligns with the book's content and appeals to the marketplace are also important. Additionally, start planning for the marketing and promotion of your book. If you've engaged a team like Stardom Books, they will support you throughout the process.

8. Publish and distribute: With all the preparation in place, it's time to publish and distribute your book. Consider your options, such as traditional publishing, self-publishing, or hybrid publishing, and choose the approach that aligns with your goals. Work with a reputable publishing partner who can handle the logistics of printing, distribution, and making your book available in various formats (e.g., print, e-book, audiobook).

9. Promote and leverage your book: After publication, focus on promoting your book to maximize its impact. Utilize various marketing strategies such as social media, speaking engagements, guest blogging, and media interviews to generate awareness and reach your target audience. Leverage your book as a powerful tool to enhance your personal brand, establish your authority, and open doors to new opportunities.

By following this structured approach, tailored specifically for startup founders, you can overcome the challenge of not knowing where to start when writing a book. Each step provides clarity and direction, ensuring that you stay focused on your purpose, audience, and key message. With the support of publishing professionals like the team at Stardom Books, you can navigate the entire process with confidence, knowing that you have expert guidance along the way.

Remember, writing a book is a rewarding endeavor that allows you to share your knowledge, experiences, and insights with a broader audience. Embrace the structured approach and embark on your writing journey, knowing that you have a roadmap to guide you toward successfully publishing your book as a startup-founder.

So, whether you're an established author like Elizabeth Gilbert seeking to elevate your craft or an industry heavyweight like Srini Rajam venturing into the realm of writing, the impact of a coach is undeniable. It's like having a trusty co-pilot on your literary expedition, ensuring you navigate the uncharted waters of writing with finesse and achieve greatness.

"The average person has around 60,000 thoughts per day - so what thoughts are you allowing to control your actions?"

Key Takeaways

To sum it up, **employing the services** of a hybrid publishing house like ours has many benefits:

- **Crafting a success strategy,** complete with distinct markers to ensure goal achievement.

- **Constructing a methodical approach** for embarking on your book-writing and publishing voyage.

- **Periodic assessment of your advancement** in relation to the established plan and adjustment as circumstances require.

- **Structuring and enhancing the content** of your book or book proposal.

- **Providing uncomplicated, efficient blueprints**, templates, or resources to accelerate your book's launch.

- **Amplifying your presence** as an author across various platforms.

- **Devising an engaging promotional strategy** for your book.

[YouTube Link](#)

11

GOING GLOBAL: REACHING INTERNATIONAL AUDIENCES AND MARKETS

"In today's interconnected landscape, your book can cross borders as effortlessly as an email—if you know how to guide its journey."

—**Raam Anand**

One of the most exciting prospects for any entrepreneur-turned-author is the possibility of extending their impact far beyond local or national boundaries. While your home market may have been your initial focus, going global can multiply both your audience and your opportunities. Whether you've written about technology, leadership, personal development, or a niche industry, there's almost certainly an international community eager for your insights.

This chapter explores the strategies, challenges, and rewards of taking your book to a worldwide readership. We'll look at the practical steps for distributing and marketing your title internationally, discuss language and cultural considerations, and examine how global reach can feed back into your entrepreneurial success. If you've ever wondered how to get your message in front of international readers, form cross-border partnerships, or land speaking gigs in multiple countries, read on.

Why Going Global Matters

Expanding Your Readership and Influence

For many entrepreneurs, writing a book is partly about *cementing* influence. Yet, if you stay confined to a single language or region, you might be missing out on a broader network of peers, customers, and fans. A strong international presence can yield:

• **New Business Opportunities**: Partnerships or joint ventures in foreign markets, including overseas companies interested in your methodology.

• **Cross-Cultural Insights**: Exposure to different ways of thinking about your topic, enriching your future work or next book.

• **Enhanced Credibility**: Being known as an "internationally recognized author" can open high-level doors—speaking engagements, consulting jobs, and more.

Leveraging the Global Shift to Digital

The internet and digital publishing platforms have drastically lowered the barriers to distributing content worldwide. A budding entrepreneur in São Paulo can discover your ebook at 2 a.m. local time just as easily as someone in your hometown. When these international readers resonate with your message, they can become brand ambassadors in their own local networks.

Diverse Revenue Streams

In addition to broader exposure, tapping into international markets can stabilize or boost your income. When one market experiences a seasonal lull or economic downturn, another might be thriving. With the right infrastructure, you can keep book sales and related revenue streams (like online courses or coaching) humming along worldwide.

Global eBook Market :[1]

• **Revenue Projections:** The global eBook market is projected to grow from approximately USD 18.2 billion in 2023 to USD 29.9 billion by 2033, reflecting a Compound Annual Growth Rate (CAGR) of 5.1% over the forecast period.

• **User Penetration:** The number of eBook users worldwide is expected to increase by approximately 92.9 million between 2024 and 2027.

Global Audiobook Market :[2]

• **Market Size and Growth:** The global audiobook market was valued at USD 6.83 billion in 2023 and is expected to reach USD 8.67 billion in 2024. Projections indicate it could grow to approximately USD 35.04 billion by 2030, with a CAGR of 26.2% from 2024 to 2030.

• **Regional Insights :**

o **North America :** In 2023, the U.S. audiobook market generated $2 billion in revenue, with 52% of adults having listened to an audiobook.

o **China :** Approximately 43% of consumers in China listen to audiobooks, indicating a significant user base in the region.

These trends highlight the increasing global adoption of digital reading and listening formats, with regional markets exhibiting unique growth patterns influenced by cultural, technological, and economic factors.

---

1. Market.us, *eBooks Market Analysis, Trends, and Growth Forecast 2023-2033*, Market.us, 2024, https://market.us/report/ebooks-market.

2. Grand View Research, *Audiobooks Market Size, Share & Trends Analysis Report 2024-2030*, Grand View Research, 2024, https://www.grandviewresearch.com/industry-analysis/audiobooks-market. Financial Times, *The Rise of Audiobooks: Market Trends and Growth Insights*, Financial Times, 2024, https://www.ft.com/content/9c2907d5-2d8a-416c-8431-168f65965493. Statista, *Share of Audiobook Users in Selected Countries Worldwide*, Statista, 2024, https://www.statista.com/forecasts/1452531/share-of-audiobook-users-in-selected-countries-worldwide.

Assessing Your Global Potential

Before you dive into new markets, take stock of whether your book's content travels well across cultural and language divides. This doesn't necessarily mean your book must appeal to *everyone everywhere*—only that the audience you do want to reach exists, and you can adapt your work suitably.

Evaluating Content Universality

- **Topic Relevance**: Does your subject—leadership strategies, personal productivity, or marketing tactics—apply globally, or is it deeply tied to localized practices?
- **Cultural Sensitivity**: Could certain anecdotes, idioms, or references misfire in other cultural contexts?
- **Timeliness vs. Timelessness**: Trends in technology or regulations differ across regions, which may limit or expand your potential audience.

Identifying Priority Markets

Going global doesn't mean attacking every country at once. Reflect on:

- **Where Your Industry is Growing**: If you're in e-commerce, for instance, you might focus on Asia-Pacific regions where e-commerce adoption is booming.
- **Existing Audience Clues**: Check your website analytics or social media followers. Are there substantial clusters of people engaging from a particular region or country already?

Translation and Localization Strategies

- **When to Translate**

Translation can be expensive and time-consuming. Consider it once you've validated strong international interest. If you have consistent social media engagement, email subscribers, or business inquiries from a non-English-speaking region, that's often your green light.

- **Selecting Languages**

Start with one or two widely spoken languages (e.g., Spanish, Mandarin, French). Alternatively, choose the language where you see a clear market fit for your niche.

- **Professional vs. Machine Translation**: While tools like Google Translate are continually improving, professional human translators (ideally with subject-matter expertise) ensure more accurate nuance and cultural appropriateness.
- **Cultural Adaptation**

Localization isn't only about language conversion. It may involve tweaking examples, references, or data points that make sense for your target culture. For example, a chapter on marketing might need local consumer trends or different case studies to resonate with readers in Japan versus Germany.

- **Currency and Measurement**: Convert dollars to local currencies, miles to kilometers, etc.

- **Examples and Jargon**: Swap out references to American baseball analogies, for instance, if addressing audiences that don't follow that sport.

- **Cover Design and Title Tweaks**

In some instances, rethinking your cover or even renaming your book for certain markets can boost appeal. Local designers or marketing consultants can help you figure out if your original design will connect or if it's culturally off-track.

HARUKI MURAKAMI'S NORWEGIAN WOOD

- **Global Distribution Channels**

Even if your book stays in English for the moment, international distribution can open you up to millions of potential new readers.

Online Retailers

Amazon's Global Marketplaces

Amazon has domain-specific marketplaces (e.g., .co.uk, .de, .co.jp), each with its own promotional tools and algorithms. By listing your book in multiple marketplaces, you increase your visibility in those regions.

- **Kindle Direct Publishing (KDP)**: Enables you to distribute eBooks and paperbacks worldwide relatively easily.
- **Amazon Advertising**: Localize your ad campaigns by language and region to better target potential readers.

Other Platforms

- **Kobo, Apple Books, Google Play Books**: All offer extensive international reach, sometimes in regions less dominated by Amazon.
- **Local E-Book Stores**: In some countries, local players (e.g., Tolino in Germany) compete strongly, so doing a bit of market-specific research can pay off.

Physical Book Distribution

1. IngramSpark

A popular print-on-demand service with global distribution networks, including local Amazon sites and bookstore catalogs.

2. Local Partnerships

If your brand or topic resonates in a certain region (like India or Brazil), consider partnering with a local publisher or distributor. They often have better relationships with local bookstores, libraries, and events.

3. International Audiobooks

With audiobooks on the rise, offering an audio version can significantly expand your global footprint, especially for English-language content. Platforms like **ACX** (for Amazon/Audible) or **Findaway Voices** distribute to dozens of retailers worldwide.

• **Multilingual Audio**: For a deeper investment, hire native speakers to narrate your translated versions, opening an entire new realm of possibilities.

Marketing to International Readers

1. Creating Region-Specific Campaigns

Rather than a generic, one-size-fits-all global campaign, tailor your marketing to the unique cultural dynamics of each target region.

• **Social Media Localization**: WeChat is central in China, LINE is popular in Japan and parts of Southeast Asia, whereas WhatsApp and Facebook remain dominant in much of Europe and Latin America.

• **Regional Influencers or Affiliates**: Collaborate with local entrepreneurs or bloggers who have established trust with your desired audience.

2. Time Zones and Launch Events

Hosting a webinar or virtual book launch? Schedule at a time that accommodates your international audience or offer multiple sessions. This consideration demonstrates inclusivity and respect for their time, while boosting global engagement.

3. SEO and International Search

Search engine optimization can shift when targeting other languages. Translating your keywords, meta descriptions, and blog content ensures search engines recognize your relevance in those markets.

• **Country-Specific Domains**: If you're serious about a particular region, a localized domain (e.g., .co.uk or .de) could help.

Overcoming Common Challenges

1. Cost-Benefit Analysis of Translation

Not every market justifies the cost and effort of localization. Conduct a pilot test by offering free or low-priced content in that language—like a short report—to gauge interest before taking the leap into full-blown translation.

• **Tip**: Gather early feedback from bilingual beta readers or fans who volunteer.

2. Piracy and Copyright Concerns

Some regions have higher rates of digital piracy. Ensure you register copyright (if not already done) in major markets and consider digital rights management (DRM) options for your eBooks.

- **Practical Advice**: While anti-piracy measures exist, the reality is that widespread pirating often occurs regardless. Focusing on robust marketing and brand-building can help offset revenue losses.

3. Cultural Missteps

Even well-intentioned authors can stumble into controversies by using insensitive examples or ignoring local etiquette.

- **Best Practice**: Engage a local cultural consultant or bilingual editor to catch potential pitfalls early.

Building an International Author Platform

1. Localized Author Website

If you're truly serious about international markets, consider building localized versions of your author website in the languages you've translated your book into. It doesn't have to be complicated or large—just enough to convey key details about your work in a user-friendly way.

- **Payment Integration**: If you plan to sell directly, ensure you support local currencies and common payment methods.

2. Global Newsletter Strategy

Segment your email list by language or region. That way, announcements for special promotions, local events, or new translations remain targeted and relevant.

- **Automated Campaigns**: For instance, when someone signs up from Germany, they receive welcome emails in German, referencing local success stories or events.

3. International Media Appearances

Research local podcasts, trade magazines, or online publications related to your topic. Offering a localized press kit—with a translated book summary and professional headshots—goes a long way in impressing international media outlets.

Networking and Speaking Opportunities Abroad

Finding Events and Conferences

1. Virtual vs. In-Person

In a digitally connected world, you can speak at conferences halfway around the globe without leaving home. However, physically traveling to these events can foster deeper connections, especially if face-to-face networking is crucial in that culture.

- **Online Platforms**: Sites like LinkedIn or specialized conference aggregators can help you discover events looking for speakers on your book's topic.
- **Local Chambers of Commerce & Business Associations**: If you're traveling to a specific country for personal or business reasons, see if you can coordinate a local speaking engagement.

2. Coordinating Book Tours or Signings

Physical book tours can still be a draw, particularly if your entrepreneurial story resonates deeply with an international community.

Best Practices

- **Identify key cities**: Focus on business hubs or cultural centers where your audience is likely concentrated.
- **Partner with local bookstores, coworking spaces, or entrepreneur groups**: They can assist with event promotions and set-up.
- **Leverage cross-promotions**: If you have local brand or sponsor partnerships, see if they can boost your event marketing.

3. Feedback Loops and Community Building

When you cross national and linguistic borders, it's essential to cultivate feedback from readers around the world. Doing so positions you to continuously improve your content and offerings, plus fosters deeper loyalty among new fans.

Encouraging Reviews and Testimonials

1. Localized Reviews

Ask readers to post reviews on the regional Amazon sites or local equivalents. Positive, genuine reviews in the local language significantly boost credibility for that market.

2. Global Reader Engagement

Hosting virtual Q&A sessions or discussion groups tailored to specific time zones can help you connect with international readers. You can also create region-specific social media groups or channels where readers can discuss your book in their native language.

3. Future Editions and Updates

If you receive consistent feedback that certain sections of your book aren't as relevant overseas, consider releasing a region-specific edition or a supplementary guide addressing local regulations, trends, or case studies.

Capitalizing on Worldwide Momentum

1. Converting Global Readers into Global Clients

The real goldmine of "going global" might not be the incremental book sales, but the people worldwide who become consulting or course clients, event attendees, or corporate partners. Keep an eye on website analytics, email open rates, and inquiry locations. If you see an uptick from a specific region, respond swiftly with localized offerings or partnerships.

2. Case in Point

An American entrepreneur who wrote a book on digital marketing found unexpected traction in Southeast Asia. By quickly partnering with a regional training institute, she launched a series of local workshops and ended up with a robust new revenue stream.

3. Licensing and Franchise Opportunities

In some fields, your methods, frameworks, or intellectual property (IP) can be licensed to other professionals or businesses abroad, akin to a franchise model. For instance, if your book explains a unique coaching methodology, you could certify coaches in different regions to use and teach your system—for a fee or revenue share.

– Key Considerations

- Ensure your IP is well-documented and protected.
- Decide on your licensing terms—flat fee, per-user fee, or tiered structure.
- Provide consistent branding, training, and marketing support to your licensees.

Action Steps: Charting Your Global Path

Here's a concise roadmap to guide you as you expand your book's impact worldwide:

1. Research & Validate

- Use website analytics and social media insights to see where potential readers are located.
- Engage local supporters or peers for initial feedback on your content's appeal and cultural fit.

2. Select Priority Markets

- Focus on the regions where there's clear demand for your topic.
- Seek out local publishers, distributors, or JV partners for market entry.

3. Plan Translation & Localization

- Work with professional translators and cultural consultants.
- Adapt references, measurements, and examples to resonate with local readers.

4. Optimize Distribution

- List on multiple Amazon marketplaces, consider global POD services.
- Explore local e-commerce or aggregator sites.

5. Localize Marketing

- Adapt social media strategies and run region-specific ad campaigns.
- Coordinate launch events or signings in target regions if feasible.

6. Build Relationships

- Seek out local media coverage, podcasts, or influencer collaborations
- Host region-focused webinars at convenient times and in relevant languages if possible.

7. Monitor & Adapt

• Track international sales, reviews, and inquiries.

• Update your strategy or content based on reader feedback, new cultural insights, and changing market dynamics.

Becoming a Truly Global Entrepreneur-Author

Reaching international audiences is far more than just a nice milestone—done thoughtfully, it can become a cornerstone of your entrepreneurial growth. The world is hungry for new ideas, fresh perspectives, and problem-solving methods. By adapting your book's message and distribution to different cultures and languages, you're not only broadening your own horizons but also empowering readers who might otherwise have never encountered your work.

"When you embrace global outreach, your words—and the ripple effect of your entrepreneurial wisdom—can cross oceans and transcend borders."
— Raam Anand

Ultimately, "going global" isn't a one-and-done move. It's an ongoing adventure where you'll discover fresh angles on your own expertise, form transformative partnerships, and expand both your business and personal worldview. With the right mix of cultural sensitivity, localized marketing, and strategic distribution, your book can become as international as the ideas and passions that sparked it in the first place.

12
PUTTING IT ALL TOGETHER

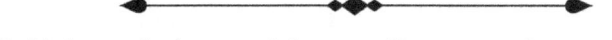

"Publishing a book is one of the most effective ways for entrepreneurs to establish their thought leadership. It's a strategic move that can enhance your brand, attract media attention, and create new business opportunities."
—**Forbes**

As we reach the end of this journey through the transformative power of writing a book, it's time to take action. You now understand how becoming an author can elevate your professional status, expand your network, enhance stakeholder relationships, boost your startup's reputation, and bring personal and professional fulfillment. These benefits are not just theoretical; they are real and achievable, as demonstrated by the numerous examples of successful startup founders who have leveraged their authorship to make a significant impact.

Let's briefly revisit the key benefits covered in this book...

1. Elevating Professional Status: Writing a book establishes you as a thought leader and expert in your field, boosting your credibility and opening doors to new opportunities.

2. Overcoming Inner Barriers: Writing a book requires overcoming self-doubt, fear of judgment, and perfectionism. This process strengthens resilience, builds confidence, and empowers you to share your expertise with the world.

3. **Expanding Your Professional Network**: A book serves as a powerful networking tool, helping you connect with potential clients, partners, investors, and influencers.

4. **Enhancing Stakeholder Relationships**: Authorship can improve communication, build trust, and foster stronger relationships with investors, clients, and employees.

5. **Boosting Your Startup's Reputation**: A well-crafted book can enhance your brand's visibility, attract media attention, and position your startup as an industry leader.

6. **Personal and Professional Fulfillment**: The process of writing a book can be deeply fulfilling, providing a sense of achievement, personal growth, and the opportunity to inspire and empower others.

7. **Handling Criticism, Feedback, and Public Reaction**: Publishing a book exposes you to public scrutiny. Learning to navigate feedback constructively enhances your credibility, improves future work, and helps you engage meaningfully with your audience.

8. **Strategic Business Growth**: A book can drive business growth by generating leads, opening new revenue streams, enhancing brand visibility, and creating strategic partnerships.

9. **Monetizing the Book Beyond Royalties**: A book can generate revenue through speaking engagements, consulting opportunities, online courses, and licensing deals, transforming it into a long-term business asset.

10. **Going Global: Reaching International Audiences and Markets**: Expanding beyond local markets allows you to connect with a diverse global audience, increase book sales, and establish an international presence in your industry.

Take the First Step

The journey to authorship begins with a single step. Whether you have a clear vision for your book or are still formulating your ideas, the most important thing is to start. Begin by outlining your key messages, identifying your target audience, and setting a realistic timeline for your writing process. Remember, you don't have to do it all at once; take it one chapter at a time, and don't hesitate to seek help from professionals who can guide you through the process.

Seek Consultation and Support

Writing a book is a significant undertaking, but you don't have to do it alone. There are numerous resources and support services available to help you succeed. Consider seeking consultation from experienced publishing advisors, ghostwriters, editors, and marketing professionals who can assist you at every stage of your authorship journey. Their expertise can make the process smoother and more efficient, ensuring that your book reaches its full potential.

Consulting with publishing experts or coaches can provide personalized insights. Amid the labyrinth of choices, a guiding light often comes in the form of professional expertise. Engaging with publishing experts or coaches allows you to navigate the terrain with seasoned insights. Their guidance offers a personalized compass, helping you decipher the nuances of each path and tailor your choices to your unique circumstances. By evaluating your goals, assessing your resources, understanding your audience, considering your genre, and seeking professional guidance, you can orchestrate a melody that resonates with your individual aspirations and creative essence.

Example: Satish Rao's "Can I Fly?"

Satish Rao's professional journey, spanning 25 years across different continents, paints a portrait of an accomplished leader. With roles on the Board of Directors as a Country/Regional Leader, Business Head, and General Manager, Rao's experience is a testament to his adept leadership and cross-functional expertise. His expertise shines through in his role in drafting and executing the 'India entry strategy' for McCormick through acquisitions and joint ventures.

In his book, *"Can I Fly?"* Satish Rao touches on a universally felt sentiment – the feeling of encountering barriers in life and career.

Rao's narrative resonates with those who've experienced the glass ceiling and questioned the fairness of opportunity distribution. His words speak to the pursuit of dreams in the face of doubt and futility. Through his own life story, Rao exemplifies that background need not be a deterrent to achieving one's aspirations.

Satish Rao's decision to embrace hybrid publishing was driven by a desire to maintain a sense of ownership over his message while accessing the expertise that a publishing house provides.

Rao's journey of bringing "Can I Fly?" to life was a collaborative effort enabled by hybrid publishing. This unique approach blended the benefits of traditional publishing with self-publishing, offering Rao both creative control and professional support.

Hybrid publishing allowed Rao to have a say in key decisions, from book design to marketing strategy. With his extensive leadership background, Rao was able to collaborate closely with professionals to create a book that aligns seamlessly with his vision.

While Rao's role in crafting his book was substantial, he was not alone in the journey. Hybrid publishing ensured that he had a team of seasoned professionals – editors, designers, and marketers – to guide and refine his work, ultimately enhancing its impact.

Through hybrid publishing, Rao was able to share his insights and inspirations with a global audience. The blend of personal anecdotes and real-life examples created a narrative that resonates with readers from various walks of life.

Satish Rao's "Can I Fly?" is a testament to how hybrid publishing can serve as a powerful bridge between authorial autonomy and professional collaboration. This publishing approach elevated Rao's message, allowing him to inspire others with his journey of transcending barriers and achieving personal and professional success.

And you may ask, what sets these authors apart and allows them to gain such substantial recognition and influence through their books? Undoubtedly, it was their extensive expertise and leadership skills in their specific fields which were key factors that contributed to their prominence. However, their accomplishments were not solely attributed to their knowledge; it was also greatly influenced by the way they chose to navigate the landscape of publishing their books.

Their success was a combination of their domain expertise and their strategic decisions in bringing their insights to the world. These authors recognized that a well-written book is not only a testament to their island of knowledge but also a powerful tool for establishing themselves as thought leaders and authorities in their fields. Through their books, they were able to share their unique perspectives, innovative ideas, and valuable experiences with a wider audience.

Furthermore, their approach to publishing was instrumental in achieving this level of recognition. They understood that the path to widespread impact involved careful consideration of the various publishing options available. Whether it was traditional publishing, self-publishing, or the hybrid approach, these authors evaluated the pros and cons of each method in light of their goals and audience.

By choosing the hybrid publishing route, they were able to target their intended readership effectively, leverage existing networks, and tap into the resources needed to enhance the visibility of their books. This strategic decision not only ensured that their messages reached the right people but also empowered them to make a lasting impact.

The success of these authors in gaining significant traction from their books was a result of their ability to marry their deep expertise with a well-thought-out publishing strategy along with their guide. It highlights the importance of not only possessing valuable knowledge but also understanding how to package and present it in a way that resonates with the intended audience. Through this synergy of expertise and strategic publishing choices, these authors were able to make a profound mark in their respective fields and beyond.

The Transformative Power of Becoming a Published Author

Becoming a published author is a transformative experience. It's an opportunity to share your knowledge and insights with the world, to leave a lasting legacy, and to make a meaningful impact on your industry and beyond. The process of writing a book challenge you to articulate your vision, reflect on your journey, and refine your ideas. It's a journey of self-discovery and growth that can profoundly change the way you see yourself and your business.

Lasting Impact on Personal and Professional Growth

The impact of writing a book extends far beyond the moment of publication. Your book will continue to influence and inspire readers long after it's released, creating a lasting legacy that contributes to your personal and professional growth. As an author, you'll have the satisfaction of knowing that your insights are making a difference, helping others navigate their own paths to success. This lasting impact is one of the most rewarding aspects of becoming a published author.

Though writing and editing a book requires a fair amount of time and research, it can have transformative results for your business. As you use your book to bolster your credibility and expand your market reach, you will be able to grow at a much faster rate than ever before. By writing a book, startup founders can build their personal brand, establish their expertise, and build trust with potential clients.

Who should write a book? Should all entrepreneurs write a book?

Well, here's a list of reasons why you SHOULD write a book:

1. You want to become a voice of authority in the field and to be the go-to person.

2. If you want to network at higher levels of engagement.

3. Enhancing the relationship with your stakeholders and improving your communication with them.

4. You want to boost sales and your reputation and get more clients on board.

5. You want to confront your personal and professional fulfillment. And the transcendent experience of leaving a legacy.

6. You want to boost your market presence and grow in a positive direction.

Publishing Possibilities

In the complex landscape of publishing possibilities, your quest to determine the ideal publishing avenue parallels the meticulous craftsmanship of tailoring a bespoke suit. It requires thoughtful consideration, informed choices, and expert guidance. This guide serves as your compass, aiding you in sculpting the publishing path that resonates with your distinctive aspirations, resources, and creative vision. To facilitate this intricate process, here's an elaborate elucidation of the essential steps and considerations meticulously designed to illuminate the right path for you:

Embarking on your publishing journey is a complex endeavor that demands careful deliberation and strategic planning. Here, we break down the steps to provide you with a roadmap for making well-informed decisions:

Define Personal Goals and Expectations: Set clear goals that align with your desired outcomes and consider success metrics. Traditional publishing supports a cohesive series, while self-publishing offers immediate authorial control. Hybrid models excel in adaptability, accommodating both visions seamlessly.

Assess Resources and Capabilities: Evaluate your budget, time, and skillset. Traditional models demand a substantial initial investment, while self-publishing requires financial allocation for editing, design, and marketing services. The hybrid approach strikes a balance by offering moderate investment for enhanced professional support.

Understand Your Target Audience: Comprehend your readers' preferences and consider their engagement channels. Self-publishing excels in adaptability, while traditional routes leverage established distribution networks. Hybrid models combine these advantages, forming a bridge between flexibility and access.

Consider Genre and Content Specifics: Consider market trends and the nature of your creation. Self-publishing thrives in niche genres, while traditional routes offer access to well-established audiences. Hybrid models synthesize genre-specific needs, ensuring your work aligns with industry trends.

Consult with Professionals: Gain insights from experts and peers by seeking guidance from publishing coaches or advisors. Author networks are invaluable, offering real-world perspectives and shedding light on the intricacies and nuances of different publishing routes.

A book assumes the role of a dynamic extension of an author's personal brand. Amidst a crowded landscape, it differentiates them, forging an identity that is uniquely theirs. The book becomes a tangible embodiment of their values, insights, and experiences, underscoring their distinctiveness in a sea of voices.

Writing a book is a journey worth embarking on. It's a powerful tool for achieving personal and professional milestones, building meaningful relationships, and driving business growth. The process may be challenging, but the rewards are immense. As you set out on this path, remember that every successful author started with a single idea and a commitment to sharing their story. Your book has the potential to change lives, starting with your own. Embrace the journey, trust in your vision, and take the first step towards becoming a published author today.

The world is in chaos. If there is anything people need right now, it is hope and help. When you publish your non-fiction story and share what you have been through, your struggles, what you have learned, or what you have overcome, you become the voice of hope and help.

People do not need ground-breaking new inventions or out-of-this-world techniques in a book. All they need is perspective, some insights, and a direction to follow. If people need information, they Google it. If they need perspective, wisdom, direction, or coaching, they need you. They need someone who has a little bit more knowledge than themselves.

They need someone who has seen it, done it, or experienced it so that they can guide them in the right direction. If you are someone who has had the idea of authoring a book but has not taken to it yet, then my friend, this is the best time for you to realize that dream. Although many people know that writing a book will change the trajectory of their lives, they just don't do it as they are not familiar with the process. Just like anybody can dance, with a little training, anybody can write a book with enough preparation and guidance. You will be scared until you dip your feet into the water. But, once you get comfortable, no one can stop you from swimming your way to the other side.

So, what are you waiting for?

Come over to our side and unlock your potential!

"Staying in touch with your readers post-launch transforms them from passive consumers into an active community, fueling ongoing support for your ideas."
—**Raam Anand**

"When I was really young, William Burroughs told me, 'Build a good name. Keep your name clean. Don't make compromises. Don't worry about making a bunch of money or being successful. Be concerned with doing good work. And make the right choices and protect your work. And if you can build a good name, eventually that name will be its own currency.'"
— **Patti Smith**

BEFORE BECOMING AN AUTHOR		AFTER BECOMING AN AUTHOR
Limited reach and recognition in professional circles and beyond.	01 VISIBILITY	Significantly expanded visibility, reaching a global audience and gaining media attention.
Expertise recognized mostly within immediate networks or industry circles.	02 CREDIBILITY	Enhanced credibility as a published author, with recognized authority in your field.
Opportunities limited to existing network and industry visibility.	03 PROFESSIONAL OPPORTUNITIES	Increased opportunities for speaking engagements, consulting, and leadership roles due to elevated status
Personal brand may blend in with peers, lacking a distinctive edge.	04 PERSONAL BRAND	Strong personal brand differentiation, showcasing expertise and unique insights through published work.
Networking efforts may require more initiative and effort to connect with industry leaders and peers.	05 NETWORKING	Networking becomes more dynamic, with new connections seeking you out for your published insights and expertise.
Primarily reliant on conventional income sources related to one's field or profession.	06 INCOME STREAMS	Diversified income potential through book sales, speaking fees, workshops, and more.
Engagement primarily through direct channels like social media, blogs, or industry events.	07 AUDIENCE ENGAGEMENT	Deeper engagement with a broader audience through the book, discussions, and related content platforms.
Professional achievements may not be widely documented or shared.	08 LEGACY	Lasting legacy through a tangible contribution to your field, impacting readers and future professionals.

"A book's true power lies in the conversation it starts—and that conversation doesn't end on launch day, but rather begins in earnest."
— **Raam Anand**

BONUS:
KEEPING MOMENTUM LONG AFTER PUBLISHING

"The launch of your book is not an ending, but a pivotal beginning—what you do next determines whether it remains a fleeting spark or ignites a lasting flame.."
—**Raam Anand**

Congratulations! You've shepherded your book from seedling idea to a fully published work—and hopefully, the launch day was met with excitement, support, and maybe even some strong initial sales or media interest. Yet for many authors, especially entrepreneur-authors, the period after the launch can feel like a drop-off. You put immense energy into pre-launch outreach, social media blitzes, perhaps a live or virtual event, and then...what comes next?

The truth is, a book's lifespan extends far beyond its initial debut. With the right strategies, you can keep it relevant, compelling, and working in tandem with your entrepreneurial goals for months—or even years—after it first hits the shelves. This chapter will explore the key activities and mindsets that help maintain momentum, whether your aim is to nurture a long-tail of steady sales, use the book as a springboard for speaking opportunities, or integrate it into your expanding business ecosystem.

Reframing the Post-Launch Mindset
1. Launch Day as a Milestone, Not the Finish Line
Many entrepreneurs approach the publication date like it's the ultimate finish line, only to discover that sustained book success (and the professional benefits that follow) rely on consistent, long-term effort. Shifting your perspective from "I made it!" to "Now the real journey begins" is essential for maintaining momentum.

Why This Mindset Matters

- **Steady Visibility**: Books rarely become overnight sensations without ongoing marketing.
- **Relationship Building**: Some of your most valuable connections—media, industry experts, new clients—arise from consistent, post-launch engagement.
- **Strategic Integration**: Your book's content can shape future products, services, and brand stories, but only if you keep nurturing it.

2. The Concept of a "Slow Burn" Success

Rather than striving for a single explosive moment—like a one-day spike in bestseller lists—consider how to cultivate a "slow burn." This means building persistent word-of-mouth, continuous updates, and multiple promotional waves that keep your book in the conversation. Entrepreneurs who take this approach often see steady sales, deeper audience loyalty, and a chance to refine their messaging as they go.

Continuing to Promote Your Book Strategically

1. Scheduling Promotional Waves

After the initial launch, plan periodic promotions or "mini-launches" every few months. These can be themed around certain seasons, tie-ins to current events, or updates to your business offerings.

Ideas for Mini-Launches

- **Anniversary Sale**: Offer the eBook or audiobook at a discount on the 6-month or 1-year anniversary of publication.
- **Holiday Tie-Ins**: Position your book as a great gift during relevant holidays or awareness months if your topic aligns.
- **New Foreword or Bonus Chapter**: Release an updated version with extra insights, case studies, or an exclusive foreword by a notable figure in your industry.

2. Tapping into Ongoing Publicity

Long-Tail Media Outreach

Don't assume all your media pitches must happen before launch. Journals, podcasts, and websites need fresh content year-round. If your topic becomes newly relevant—say, a big industry shift or trending conversation—reach out with your unique perspective drawn from the book.

• **Recurring Columns**: Secure a guest-column slot in a publication where you can frequently reference your book's core ideas.

• **Podcasts and Webinar Appearances**: Keep an eye out for new shows in your niche, or set up recurring appearances on popular channels that you developed rapport with during your pre-launch phase.

Conference Panels and Speaking Gigs

Industry conferences often book speakers months in advance. If you didn't land a slot during your launch period, keep reaching out. Show organizers love authors with a proven track record of thought leadership—your post-launch reviews, testimonials, and sales figures can strengthen your pitch.

Integrating Your Book into Your Business Ecosystem

1. As a Lead Magnet or Customer Touchpoint

Free or Discounted Copies

Rather than treating your book as a stand-alone item, you could bundle a digital copy (or discounted print version) with your existing products or services. This approach exposes your ideas to more people, potentially converting casual buyers into long-term followers.

• **Webinar Registrations**: Offer the book as a bonus for those who sign up for your paid webinars or masterclasses.

• **Onboarding Gift**: For new clients, especially high-ticket ones, a signed copy can create a personal connection.

2. Repurposing Book Content Across Platforms

Blog Series

Take each chapter—or a segment thereof—and expand it into a dedicated blog post. Link back to the full book, encouraging deeper exploration of the topic.

Podcasts and Mini-Videos

Record short videos that highlight a key framework or anecdote from your book. Publish them on LinkedIn, YouTube, or Instagram. This type of "micro-content" can pique curiosity among those who haven't read your work yet.

3. Creating Spin-Off Products

Courses, Workshops, and Coaching

If your book resonates with a particular audience segment, they might want a more direct or guided experience. Turn your chapters into modules for an online course, an interactive workshop, or a short-term group coaching program. This not only enhances your authority but also brings in additional revenue streams (as covered in previous chapters on monetizing beyond royalties).

Private Membership Community

Establish a community—on a platform like Facebook Groups, Slack, or a specialized membership site—where readers can discuss the book's lessons. You can host monthly Q&A sessions, bring in guest experts, and further solidify your brand as an ongoing resource.

Gathering and Showcasing Social Proof

1. Encouraging Reviews and Testimonials

Why Ongoing Reviews Matter

You might have collected a flurry of reviews at launch, but fresh feedback signals relevance to new readers. A steady influx of testimonials keeps your book listing or website from looking outdated.

Strategies

- **Automated Email Nudges**: If you captured readers' emails through a lead magnet, follow up politely with a request for a review once they've had time to read.

- **Social Media Calls to Action**: Periodically remind followers that reviews help others discover the book.

- **Review Swaps**: In some entrepreneurial communities, authors form alliances—reading and reviewing one another's books ethically, providing constructive feedback.

2. Gathering Case Studies

If your book presents practical tools, frameworks, or advice, a certain percentage of readers will use them with remarkable success. Proactively invite them to share their stories.

- **Written Testimonials**: Perfect for newsletters, landing pages, or press kits.
- **Video Interviews**: Offer to interview a reader via Zoom or other platforms about their transformation after applying your methods.
- **Before-and-After Snapshots**: If relevant (e.g., financial growth, weight loss, or operational improvements), a compelling visual can emphasize the impact of your book's ideas.

Planning and Executing Updates or Next Editions

1. The Rationale for Revised Editions

As an entrepreneur, you're probably updating your ideas in real time. Maybe a tool you recommended in your original manuscript has since been replaced, or an industry shift demands a new approach. A revised edition (or even an extended workbook) can help you maintain accuracy and relevance.

Benefits

- **Renewed Launch Opportunities**: Treat your revised edition almost like a new book—complete with fresh marketing pushes.
- **Media Hooks**: Journalists appreciate updated content that relates to current events or ongoing trends.
- **Evergreen Accuracy**: Ensuring your book remains up-to-date can reduce negative reviews that stem from outdated information.

2. Adding Extras and Bonuses

If you don't feel the need for a full revision, consider adding bonus materials—like an extended chapter, new introduction, or additional case studies. Digital versions can be updated relatively quickly, and if you have print on demand, you can integrate small changes without a large reprint cost.

Potential Extras

- **Bonus Chapter**: Introduce advanced topics that you only touched on in the original.

- **Compiled FAQs**: Convert common questions from readers into an expanded Q&A section.
- **Interviews or Roundtables**: Summaries of your conversations with industry experts since your book's release.

Engaging with Your Community Over Time

1. Live Reading Sessions or AMA (Ask Me Anything) Events

Virtual Events

Even after months of being published, consider hosting an online reading session—like a book club meeting—where you read excerpts and answer real-time questions. This fosters a deeper, more personal connection.

In-Person Meetups

If possible, organize or attend events where you can autograph books and chat directly with readers. This approach can be integrated with your speaking gigs or existing conferences.

2. Regular Newsletters or Updates

If you've built an email list from your book's launch (perhaps by offering a download code or workbook in exchange for email addresses), continue nurturing that audience. A monthly or quarterly newsletter can keep them informed about:

- **Your upcoming events**
- **New content related to the book's topic**
- **Success stories or user tips from readers**

Make sure each newsletter includes a subtle invitation to share your book or connect with you through social media, reinforcing that the conversation is ongoing.

Monitoring Your Metrics and Adapting

1. Sales and Ranking Trends

Checking your book's sales data and category rankings periodically can reveal patterns. Perhaps you see a spike whenever you speak at a webinar or appear on a podcast. This helps you prioritize which activities yield the best ROI.

2. Audience Demographics

Analytics from your website, social media, or email subscribers can hint at shifting reader demographics. Maybe you notice a growing interest from a specific geographic region or an unexpected age bracket. Use these insights to tailor future content, consider translations, or craft specialized offers.

3. Feedback Loops

Monitor reviews and direct emails for emerging commonalities. If multiple readers request deeper coverage of a particular subtopic, that's a potential blog series or entire new project. If recurring complaints emerge, address them proactively—possibly in your communications or an updated edition.

Staying Relevant as an Entrepreneur-Author

4. Aligning Your Personal Growth with the Book's Core Themes

As you evolve in your entrepreneurial journey—whether launching new ventures, pivoting your business model, or deepening your expertise—draw parallels back to your book. Publicly reflect on how your latest experiences enhance or refine the ideas you originally published. This openness keeps your content dynamic and your audience engaged.

5. Creating a Loyal "Brand Orbit"

Your book should become a constant reference point in your broader brand narrative, rather than a relic overshadowed by new projects. Link back to it in interviews, keep a short blurb in your email signature, or reference it when discussing related topics on LinkedIn. The goal is to keep your book as part of your "brand orbit," revolving in synergy with all your other offerings and achievements.

Action Plan for Sustained Momentum

1. Map Out a Year of Micro-Promotions

- **Every Quarter:** Identify a theme or angle (a new event, holiday, or relevant trend) to refresh your marketing efforts.
- **Monthly Check-Ins:** Evaluate if any recent news or personal experiences tie back to your book's topic. Share these reflections publicly.

2. Host a Post-Launch Event (Real or Virtual)

- **Within 3–6 Months:** Invite readers to a celebratory "post-launch" to discuss insights, address questions, and get personalized advice from you.

3. Develop a Content Repurposing Calendar

- List each chapter's major points.
- Plan how you'll transform them into blog posts, short videos, social graphics, and newsletter features.

4. Solicit and Showcase Social Proof

- **Case Studies:** Ask readers who benefited from your advice to share tangible results.
- **Review Reminders:** Periodically encourage your email list or social followers to leave an honest review.

5. Consider an Update or Companion Product

- By the 6- or 12-month mark, reevaluate whether you need a second edition or a complementary guide, workbook, or exclusive webinar series.

6. Monitor Analytics

- **Track** sales platforms, web traffic, email sign-ups, and social engagement to identify what truly drives your ongoing momentum.

Cultivating a Long-Term Book Legacy

Publishing a book is a milestone of which any entrepreneur can be proud. However, it's the continuous nurturing—long after the publication date—that transforms a fleeting release into a sustained legacy. With deliberate promotions, fresh content, community engagement, and strategic integration into your wider business or personal brand, your book can remain a living, evolving asset.

By taking the long view, you'll give your message the time and space to permeate the market, discover new audiences, and evolve alongside your entrepreneurial journey. The ultimate reward? A deeply resonant brand, a strong reader community, and an enduring impact that outlasts the hype of any single launch day.

NEXT STEPS...

"Great brands and great businesses have to be great storytellers, too. We have to tell stories – emotive, compelling stories – and even more so because we're nonfiction."
—**Angela Ahrendts**

Don't miss out on your chance to shine.

Follow the steps for a comprehensive understanding of how we can help you flourish as a start-up though leader.

Click the links below to kickstart your authorship journey:

Step 1: www.stardombooks.com/baas.

This is a downloadable link on how to use your book as a strategy.

Step 2: stardomcircle.com

This is a community of other aspiring and growth-oriented leaders that can be useful.

Your success story starts here!

Cheers to our future.

Success isn't just about having the best product, service, or expertise—it's about being the best-known authority in your field. As the video highlights, visibility, credibility, and influence are what truly set industry leaders apart. And one of the most powerful ways to establish that authority? Writing your own book.

Your journey doesn't end here—it's just beginning. Take the next step toward positioning yourself as a thought leader:

ABOUT THE AUTHOR

Raam Anand
2-times Bestselling Author
Publishing Advisor to Top Leadership
Investor in Various Start-ups
Chief Editor & Publisher
High-performance Coach

Raam Anand coaches aspiring authors and non-writers to become published authors. He is a three-time international bestselling author and one of the most globally respected leadership coaches.

As the Chief Editor at Stardom Books (USA/India), Raam has published more than 260 books while coaching people on productivity, personal branding, and book publishing. Official statistics and magazines report that Raam is one of the world's leading publishing coaches.

He built multiple businesses in North America and Asia grossing several million dollars in revenue.

He trained hundreds of thousands of CXO's, experts, entrepreneurs, and thought leaders through his books, online courses, workshops, and conferences.

Raam spent over two decades researching and coaching on business and high-performance to present the best strategies for improving your life and career.

www.ingramcontent.com/pod-product-compliance
Lightning Source LLC
LaVergne TN
LVHW011420080426
835512LV00005B/179